CW01467908

THE GESTALT CENTRE
15 - 23 ST PANCRAS WAY
LONDON NW1 0PT

A Gestalt Institute
of Cleveland
publication

CRAZY HOPE
AND FINITE
EXPERIENCE

Crazy Hope and Finite Experience

Final Essays
of Paul Goodman

———

Taylor Stoehr, editor

Jossey-Bass Inc. • San Francisco

A Gestalt Institute of Cleveland publication

Substantial discounts on bulk quantities of Jossey-Bass books are available to corporations, professional associations, and other organizations. For details and discount information, contact the special sales department at Jossey-Bass Inc., Publishers. (415) 433-1740; Fax (415) 433-0499.

For international orders, please contact your local Paramount Publishing International office.

Manufactured in the United States of America. Nearly all Jossey-Bass books and jackets are printed on recycled paper that contains at least 50 percent recycled waste, including 10 percent postconsumer waste. Many of our materials are also printed with either soy- or vegetable-based ink; during the printing process these inks emit fewer volatile organic compounds (VOCs) than petroleum-based inks. VOCs contribute to the formation of smog.

Library of Congress Cataloging-in-Publication Data

Goodman, Paul, 1911–1972.
    Crazy hope and finite experience : final essays of Paul Goodman / [edited by] Taylor Stoehr. — 1st ed.
      p.   cm. — (Jossey-Bass social and behavioral science series)
    ISBN 0-7879-0016-8
    I. Stoehr, Taylor, date.   II. Title.   III. Series.
PS3513.O527C73   1994
814'.52—dc20
                                          94-10315
                                            CIP

FIRST EDITION
HB Printing   10 9 8 7 6 5 4 3 2 1   Code 9497

Contents

Sources and Acknowledgments

"WITHIN MY HORIZON," "Politics Within Limits," and "Beyond My Horizon—Words" form the prose portion of *Little Prayers and Finite Experience*, posthumously published by Harper & Row in 1972. "Being Queer" was originally written for a special issue of *WIN* (November 15, 1969). The revised version printed here did not appear until after Goodman had died, in *Nature Heals: The Psychological Essays of Paul Goodman*, published by Free Life Editions in 1977. "Apology for Literature" was adapted from the final chapters of *Speaking and Language* and printed in *Commentary* (July 1971) shortly before *Speaking and Language* was issued by Random House. I am grateful to the original editors and publishers for permission to reprint these five essays. I also wish to thank John Dings, Geoffrey Gardner, Naomi Goodman, Sally Goodman, Susan Goodman, Ruth Perry, and Gordon Wheeler for their helpful comments and good advice.

Cambridge, Massachusetts   Taylor Stoehr
June 1994

CRAZY HOPE
AND FINITE
EXPERIENCE

INTRODUCTION

Taylor Stoehr

PAUL GOODMAN'S PERIOD OF FAME lasted twelve years, from the publication of *Growing Up Absurd* in 1960 until his death in 1972. He was celebrated as a social critic and the young radicals of the New Left read him for his "utopian essays and practical proposals," as the title of one of his books put it. Yet, whatever his public saw in him, Goodman considered himself primarily an artist rather than a political thinker or sociologist, and many of his books, even during the sixties, were works of poetry, drama, and fiction. Perhaps his greatest single work—certainly he thought so—was *The Empire City*, a vast comic novel he had devoted a dozen years of his life to. He had also written books of literary criticism, like *Art and Social Nature*, *Kafka's Prayer*, and *The Structure of Literature*, and toward the end of his life he produced *Speaking and Language*, a telling critique of the various linguistic theories then in vogue. He had collaborated with his architect brother, Percival Goodman, on numerous treatments of architectural topics, including *Communitas*, a lively study of community planning that has become a classic, still in print after forty years. Then again, he joined with Frederick (Fritz) Perls and Ralph F. Hefferline on

Gestalt Therapy, still the primary text of the new synthesis in psychotherapy that has become an international movement. Psychotherapy, community planning, linguistics, literary theory, philosophy, sociology, politics, education, media criticism, as well as poems, plays, and fiction—thirty or forty books, depending on whether one counts posthumously published works. With such a range it was fitting that Goodman insisted on calling himself "an old-fashioned man of letters."

Very few writers in our age of specialization have taken so broad a prospect as their concern, and some of his critics thought Goodman spread himself too thin; but he never pretended to be an expert in all these areas, only an interested party, an artist with good habits of analysis and an inquiring attitude toward experience, and with a belief that "the nature of things is not easily divided into disciplines" anyway. He used to say that he really had only one subject, "the human beings I know in their man-made scene." Or again, thinking of his work as a "program," he said he was trying to understand "How to take on Culture without losing Nature."

It should be added that Goodman was not a man barricaded behind his books, nor did he ever settle into the familiar routines of professionals. Although he sometimes taught for a semester or two—every age of student, he boasted, from six to sixty—he did not play the pedagogue cloistered with his pupils. He practiced psychotherapy for ten years, yet he was never booked all day with patients. And during the sixties, when he wore himself out giving speeches to New Left audiences on a hundred campuses, he was not one to beat the shortest track from airport to lecture hall to faculty club. Someone once dubbed him a "street philosopher," and indeed he spent much of

2

his ordinary day on the pavement of his native city, Manhattan, where he knew the "routes and courses," as his college chums used to call them, like the back of his hand.

Goodman was a family man and raised three children, but he was bisexual, and in his psychic economy it was the homo-erotic impulse that dominated his fantasy life and often drew him into the streets where he cruised for sex among friends and strangers. This was a passion that was out of control—not his sexual orientation itself but his obsession with the "hunt"—and yet the hunt provided occasions for many incidental and re-warding encounters. His life was certainly full enough without this neurotic search, "looking for love where it can't be found," as he characteristically phrased it. Besides his family and his art, Goodman had many satisfying pursuits of the sort that any lively bohemian of his day might have enjoyed, though perhaps the range of his friends and interests was unusual. He played hand-ball with Puerto Rican teenagers on outdoor courts or against a convenient brick wall; he hung around the actors of The Living Theatre, especially if they were rehearsing one of his plays; he had a weekly poker date in Hoboken, New Jersey; he dropped in at the War Resisters League or the office of *Liberation* maga-zine where he was one of the editors; he walked the dog and sat on the local school board; he taught himself to play the piano and composed songs and dances; he summered at the beach or in the country, gardening and swimming; he motorcycled in Italy and Ireland and drank in the Vermeers in Amsterdam; he picketed the draft board; he ran therapy groups; he gave little talks on the radio and wrote angry letters to the mayor; he took lonely walks along the banks of the Hudson; if his friends stopped by, he was always free for their enterprises.

The fact that most of these activities could take on an erotic aura at any moment was not necessarily a drawback. Goodman wrote the equivalent of a book a year during his adult life. His extraordinary literary output cannot be explained by any single factor, but eros surely played a part, as it obviously did in his overlapping careers as a teacher, a psychotherapist, and a public man. Success came slow and late, an uphill struggle. Perhaps it was because of his compulsive sexual longing that Goodman himself never doubted there would be energy for his next step, no matter how much the world might seem determined to thwart his desires. Near the end of his life, after he had had his fill of successes as well as failures, and his obsession was also much abated, he looked back and tried to make sense of it all, not in an autobiographical mood but rather as a veteran contemplates the past, thinking what lessons might be worth passing on to those who come after. Many years earlier Goodman had written a little meditation that he titled "On the Question: 'What Is the Meaning of Life?'" He had begun by saying that no one who is happy asks such a question, and then admitted that his own unhappy answer had often been that "sexual love is the meaning of life." Were he less miserable, he added, it was probable that he would be less likely to make that answer. He was right. When he finally came to setting down his last words on the meaning of life, sexual love certainly had its place but it did not usurp the whole of his imagination. There was much else to experience and to hope for.

The five essays in *Crazy Hope and Finite Experience* may be said to constitute Goodman's parting words to the world. Three of these essays originally made up the "Finite Experience" section of Goodman's posthumously published *Little Prayers and*

Finite Experience, a hybrid work, half poems ("Little Prayers") and half *pensées*. (The little prayers will soon be reprinted in a volume of Goodman's selected poems.) The remaining two essays included here were written with the same intent as the essays of finite experience and at about the same time, a time when Goodman knew he was dying.

The last words of exemplary men and women are always of interest, in this case particularly so because Goodman meant to be offering us here an informal compendium of his ideas and attitudes, an account of how he held them and what they meant to him. He was not an old man when he gathered in this harvest, but he was wise in experience, proven by trials and deeds, and resolved to make sense of his story for those who wanted to hear it. To find near equivalents in American literature we would have to go back to the letters Thomas Jefferson and John Adams wrote to one another in their old age, or the twilight ruminations of Herman Melville in *Billy Budd*. Actually there is nothing quite like Goodman's final thoughts in our short literary tradition.

In this introduction I want to say something about the circumstances in which Goodman wrote these thoughts and also to draw attention to certain themes in them, particularly the idea of finite experience itself and the notion that emerges as its concomitant, the other side of the phenomenological coin as it were, crazy hope. Finite experience is the titular subject of the core set of three essays, with which the present book begins: "Within My Horizon," "Politics Within Limits," and "Beyond My Horizon—Words." In these essays, Goodman tells us that he is uncomfortable with abstraction and feels at home only in the here and now. His "politics within limits," described in the second essay, is grounded in this pragmatism. Crazy hope enters into the third essay's account of the world "beyond my horizon," where Goodman introduces the phrase to characterize kinds of transcendence that tempted him to abandon the finite and concrete in experience—love and art. Although he speaks of these longings in his three "Finite Experience" essays, a much fuller discussion of them is contained in the two others I have added, and so the new title, I hope, is appropriate.

Goodman was sixty years old, recuperating from a heart attack but aware that in his family they died young, when he turned to the task of summing up what life had taught him. Students often asked him, "How have *you* made it? How does one go about it?" Having agreed to spend the academic year 1971–72 at the University of Hawaii, he decided to offer a course in which he would try to describe his "way of being" for the students. Had there been no course and no students, he would have found some other excuse to set down these thoughts, for the urge was strong in him to pass on his lessons and say his farewells.

He wrote the copy for the dust jacket of *Little Prayers and Finite Experience*, speaking of himself in the third person as if already freed from the burden of being Paul Goodman, and describing himself as

> an artist and a citizen, coping with life and now aging, in poor health, and not very happy. He sees his life as having been continually hungry, balked, and poor, but never starved, nor a total failure, nor with nothing. He has not had enough courage and patience to live this purgatory well, but he has had enough to survive and to feel tested rather than damned. He has faith that he has a world-for-him, such as it is.

6

...Goodman chooses (and is stuck with) experience that is concrete and limited; its terms are Here, Now, and Next, and Darkness beyond the horizon. So in his politics, sociology, and psychology he tries to restore the matrix of primary experience in a society bedeviled, in his opinion, by political, social, and moral abstractions. From this point of view, the book is a phenomenology of what he sometimes calls "anarchism" and sometimes "neolithic conservatism."

Goodman's life *had* been hard, and he was certainly prone to complain about it, but his parting words were not self-justifying or self-righteous. He wanted to explain what sort of person he was and how he viewed the world, not what disasters had happened to make him that way.

The cruelest blow life had dealt Goodman was the accidental death of his son Mathew, almost exactly five years before he himself died. No loss affected him so catastrophically. Not long before Mathew's death, Goodman's friend Paul Weisz had died of a heart attack in front of Goodman's eyes, and others had died since. He had given the memorial speech for his collaborator on *Gestalt Therapy*, Fritz Perls. Next to his son's grave in New Hampshire he had buried the ashes of his sister, Alice, who had been a second mother to him. Warnings of the end, all of them, but Matty's loss was a wrench after which there could be none greater, not even his own looming fate—and Goodman *was* afraid of death. It was as he said in the following little prayer:

> I have no further grief in me.
> I can imagine, no, foresee
> the losses I will suffer yet,
> but my eyes do not get wet.

> When once the brass is burnished, Sire,
>   there is no use of further fire,
>   it is a mirror. But it can be melted,
>   Sire, and destroyed.

Mourn as he did, he could not work through or shake off this grief; he simply had to live with it, and it lies beneath the elegiac mood of his meditations in Hawaii. From early manhood Goodman had lived in superstitious dread of some "fatal blow," as he called it, an impending disaster he sometimes seemed to court — by declaring his homosexuality publicly, by defying the state and its conscription for war, by brandishing his nonconformity in the faces of publishers and readers alike. "Let's have it over with!" he was saying. After Mathew's death in 1967 he no longer seemed braced against this doom. His last works are without any such defiance or bravado.

As I have mentioned, Goodman called his final book *Little Prayers and Finite Experience* because, in addition to his credo, he included over a hundred poems like the one just quoted, printed on the *verso* pages while his essays appeared on the *rectos*. These little prayers also expressed what it was like to be Paul Goodman. They had long been his way of "saying at certain moments just how it was, however it was.... Evidently, when I undertake to cope with the despair, horror, joy, or confusion of my existence by writing how it is, I am bound to do so in eight four-beat lines rimed a-a, b-b, c-c, and d-d." These poems are not reprinted here because the present aim is to draw together Goodman's prosier wisdom — to look into his brassy mirror but not to feel the heat of the melting fire. But one of his little prayers stands at the head of each section of this new book, to remind the reader how the brass was burnished.

As I have said, "Finite Experience" was not the only attempt Goodman made to sum up the lessons of his life. I have added "Being Queer" and "Apology for Literature," two slightly earlier essays which are part of the same unburdening, so that there are five essays in all: on experience, politics, religion, eros, and art. One might well compare them to the essays of Ralph Waldo Emerson a century earlier on the same eternal themes, for Goodman was part of the Emersonian tradition as it comes down through the pragmatists—William James, John Dewey, Randolph Bourne—American men of letters who were not embarrassed by the summons of philosophy to make sense of what life brought them and, noblesse oblige, to speak it in the public forum instead of squirreling it away in learned journals read only by scholars.

If Goodman had any particular model in mind, however, it was probably Franz Kafka's Aphorisms, those earnest musings on paradise lost for which he himself had once provided an elaborate commentary in *Kafka's Prayer* (1947). Indeed, he spoke of "Finite Experience" as a set of "aphorisms," and in their original publication he gave them numbers, just as Kafka had numbered his "Reflections on Sin, Pain, Hope, and the True Way." Readers will notice other parallels with traditional wisdom literature—by Kierkegaard, Nietzsche, or Goodman's favorite, Lao-tzu. I myself like to think of "Finite Experience" as a twentieth-century American match for William Cobbett's crusty *Advice to Young Men*, although I doubt that Goodman had ever heard of this old self-help tract. He would have admired Cobbett's plainspoken prose, and smiled at the hectoring manner he himself had often adopted in playing Dutch uncle to the youth movement.

In his parting words, however, Goodman's voice rings pure, no cajoling or provocation in it, and no rivalrous echo of his own oracles. He was beyond all that. Although students might still provide an occasion for a speech or a book, he had grown progressively estranged from the world of the young. For ten years he had been squawking about their plight. "Go tell Aunt Rhody," he wrote at last, "the old gray goose is dead":

Oh the number of the speeches I have made
is like the witch-grass in the garden
and the press-conferences for peace
have been almost as many as the wars.
But now my stare is fixed, my blood congeals:
he asks me for another essay on the schools,
his letter flutters from my nerveless fingers.
She died in the mill pond, she died in the mill pond,
she died in the mill pond standing on her head.

Since 1968 a new generation had been leading the New Left away from its original core of existentialist ethics and anarchist tactics. To be sure, there was still a large nonviolent core of peace activists in the movement—perhaps a majority—but the ideological drift of the new leadership toward state socialism, capped by the fascination with violence and ruthless infighting of the Students for a Democratic Society (SDS), the Progressive Labor Party (PLP), and the Weatherman vanguardists, brought to Goodman's love affair with the young a fatal chill. In 1969 he wrote one more book of social criticism,

New Reformation, a final outcry in the spirit of John Wycliffe and Jan Hus at the breakdown of humane culture and traditional institutions, and a warning that his country faced a "crisis of legitimacy." Not only did he chastise the current American version of the Whore of Babylon, but he also had stern words for the young zealots whose "fanaticism and self-righteous violence" reminded him of "Luther's and Cromwell's bullies."

Having said all that, Goodman appended to *New Reformation* a little coda that he called "Notes of a Neolithic Conservative." Here we see him stepping back from polemics and speaking to posterity, already adopting the aphoristic style of "Finite Experience" and affirming many of the same attitudes, often in the very same language, though his Erasmian manner had not yet become habit.

Goodman did not say why he had chosen to declare his neolithic conservatism in this rather unusual way. At one level it was obvious enough; he was answering his critics, nailing his twenty theses to the church door. More deeply though, perhaps not even he knew why he was thinking so phenomenologically about his politics. He had written "Notes of a Neolithic Conservative" in August 1969, the second anniversary of his son's death. Within a few months he published a second such statement, this time for *WIN* magazine, put out by a group of activists from the War Resisters League. The editorial collective had invited him to contribute to a special issue on homosexuality, and they printed his response as their lead story, "Memoirs of an Ancient Activist." His photo was on the cover, along with a troubling sentence from his essay, a sentence actually first printed in "Notes of a Neolithic Conservative": "*My homosexual needs have made me a nigger.*"

11

Although Goodman had been open about his bisexuality for almost forty years, there was an aura of confession or exposée in the way the editors presented his essay, side by side with a painfully honest "coming out" by David McReynolds, and against the background of "gay pride" then sweeping Greenwich Village. Goodman had written many poems and stories about being queer, all of them autobiographical, so that despite his having never taken it up as a separate subject of inquiry and analysis, there was very little left to confess. When Goodman revised this essay later he called it "The Politics of Being Queer," a more appropriate characterization of Goodman's effort to assess his experience as a despised and excluded "nigger" of sexuality. (Here in this new edition I have abbreviated it to "Being Queer.")

In the essay he interpreted his political stance as "a willed reaction-formation" to the denial of his right to his own sexual impulses: "My plight has given energy to my anarchism, utopianism, and Gandhianism." But he did not dwell on his sufferings and there is no hint of the self-pity that suffused his journal entries in the late fifties, when he was struggling with the consequences of his passion. No doubt the intervening years had diminished his sexual need, but more than that, he seems to have arrived at a stage of nonattachment. However we explain it, "Being Queer" is an extraordinary achievement. I know no other work that makes the case for homosexual practices at once so personally and so dispassionately, not merely citing the pedagogic function of eros but also calling attention to the "profoundly democratizing" tendency of promiscuity, the "happy property of sexual acts" in breaking down squeamishness and other constraints on spontaneity, and even the way

12

that, as Goodman says, "the hardship and starvation of my inept queer life have usefully simplified my notions of what a good society is." Of course the advent of AIDS has changed some of the basic conditions for his assessment. Goodman would have had something instructive to say about that too.

As I have noted, "Being Queer" begins with sentences and an anecdote already printed in the "Notes of a Neolithic Conservative" that ended *New Reformation*. Further additions to Goodman's credo contain many other passages that had their first airing there. Goodman's next book, *Speaking and Language*, published in 1971, concluded in direct imitation of *New Reformation*'s ending. "Notes for a Defence of Poetry" was a similar series of aphoristic pronouncements rounding out the argument of *Speaking and Language* by shifting the ground to personal experience. This essay he also published separately in a somewhat different form, under the title "Apology for Literature," the version followed here. Both titles reflect Goodman's pride in joining the long tradition of poets like Sir Philip Sidney and Percy Bysshe Shelley who sang the praises of their art, though he does not take their high prophetic tone or "make their exaggerated claims," he says, "since I am just describing my own situation."

This last disclaimer draws attention again to the limited, "finite," perspective of Goodman's final pronouncements. A refrain that occurs over and over is "How would I know?"—as in, "Maybe I am lonely more than average—how would I know?" or, "Since [the young dissidents] do not know concretely enough what they mean by 'just human,' they need a tangible adversary to give themselves shape. (But how, at my age, would I know what they mean?)"

In "Finite Experience" Goodman often comes to a similar pause. For a man who always had all the answers (one of his fellow editors at *Liberation* once said that he had too much of the problem solver in him) it marked a great change when he began to repeat this formula, shrugging his shoulders and opening his hands. At one point he speaks of "an essential ignorance that clouds experience" and "gives me a headache until I find the missing clue." That was the problem-solving bent, to be distinguished from "an essential ignorance in which I float happily, and that even seems to brighten what I do know, by contrast." Unlike his politics and social thought, the practice of his literary art had always veered between these poles. And now, when it came to sage advice about the Way, like Lao-tzu Goodman sometimes had to report: "All have smiles on their faces, as if going up to the Spring Festival . . . only I am murky and confused."

Goodman wrote his "Apology for Literature" in the spring of 1971, when he was experiencing bouts of vertigo that led him to consult a specialist. By the time it was published the following winter he had had his first heart attack. It was an unusually hot day in Northern New Hampshire when it happened, and he had been tearing down a dilapidated chicken house in the field next to the old farmhouse at the Goodmans' summer place. Later he had joined family and friends for croquet, a traditionally genteel game which he, however, played with such childish competitiveness—he was not above cheating—that people used to stamp off the lawn swearing never to play with him again. "I ought to have worn a hat," he said in *Little Prayers and Finite Experience*.

Characteristically, he dealt with his health crisis in little prayers:

An hour of panic while I fight
for breath, and then all night
   in detail, rib by rib,
   exquisitely my muscles pick

themselves apart, until at dawn
I sink exhausted down.
   No doubt, Lord, though I do not see,
   that this is useful to me.

When the invitation came to spend the following year in
Hawaii, it seemed like a good idea. The university would not ask
much of him, and he could swim—cautiously—in the blue
Pacific just outside his door. "Finite Experience" would be part of
his convalescence. After setting down his thoughts on his "way
of being," he planned to go through his little prayers and arrange
them in a final sequence for the other half of the "book on religion" he had promised to write. The publishers probably expected some further "Protestant" interpretations of the protest
movements of the day, like those in New Reformation, but he was
finished with that kind of social criticism. After Little Prayers and
Finite Experience he decided to read through all his poems and
make a collected edition of them. He had already brought his
short stories together in Adam and His Works in 1969. A second
heart attack in the spring made it clear there would not be much
time to spare. He had almost finished harvesting his poems when
he had his third, and final, attack, August 2, 1972. In another
month he would have been sixty-one years old.

   In spite of the context I have sketched out, "Finite
Experience" was not a meditation on mortality. Goodman had

15

a horror of death; he did not want to talk about it even if he could not stop dreading it. Although inured to pain and quite puritanical about anodynes and anesthetics, he had always been a physical coward, quick to panic when cornered or constrained. But his habitual moral courage stood firm. He faced resolutely toward life and dutifully filed his report.

Because he had already written about eros and art in the essays just discussed, these topics were not given sections of their own in "Finite Experience," but neither were they excluded from the three divisions of life he addressed himself to there: how he experienced the world, the politics that followed from that kind of experience, and what he hoped or believed beyond experience. There was plenty of elbow room in such categories, and he made no attempt to keep things systematic. If he spoke in his first essay of how he coped with tragic conflicts "such as a loyalty to contradictory absolute values," he did not feel bound to avoid talking about the same ultimate dilemmas in his third essay, where he repeats his observation that "the recipe of our Greek tragic plots is decently to affirm both contradictions, to sink into them deeper, till the protagonist becomes exhausted and then confused and then goes blank, all with a good conscience." He also obviously enjoyed the opportunity to reiterate many of his favorite sayings, the wisdom he had borrowed from others or discovered for himself over forty years and more. Concluding his remarks on tragic conflict, for instance, he quotes Rabbi Tarfon, whose uncomfortable advice he had been repeating for at least twenty-five years: "You do not need to finish the task, but neither are you free to leave it off."

He knew he was repeating himself; that was the point. Thus, on another page, he says, "In a passage that I often repeat,

Goethe speaks of that patient finite thing the Earth. 'The poor Earth!—I evermore repeat it—a little sun, a little rain, and it grows green again.' It has a tonic effect on us. So the Earth repeats it, Goethe repeats it, and I repeat it."

Goodman had many such touchstones kept polished by frequent use. Since 1934 he had been quoting Aristotle's dictum that "when sensory power is actualized, when there *is* experience, the sense organ is the *same as* the sensed object." In Goodman's view, this was the central insight of *Gestalt Therapy*, and he had begun the theoretical portion of that book with his explanation, repeated in his essays, that both the "I" of the organism and the "that there" of the environment are abstractions, coming after the primary fact of experience itself. In "Finite Experience" he offered a personal illustration of these dynamics—"I myself usually pay attention after I have had an insight rather than to produce one, for it is easier to attend to what is interesting, what is becoming interesting"—but it was the same point about self and experience that he had made in *Gestalt Therapy* and in passages he had written on aesthetic theory a dozen years before that.

There were also puzzles and cruxes he found irresistible. In his diary of the fifties, *Five Years*, he had asked himself whether there was not some important truth obscured by the scientific principle of the conservation of energy. In fields like literature or psychotherapy, for instance, such a principle made no sense; perhaps in natural science it was also misleading, however "true." He returns twice in "Finite Experience" to the question whether "the physicists who affirm conservation are not using it as an *a priori* principle, proving it beforehand by their language of equations and by their attitude toward the matter they

17

work on." A Taoist physics of "the fertile void" might even be technologically productive—who knows? I think it amused him to deny entropy as his own life ran down. And yet he was also fond of saying, "Nothing comes from nothing."

He noticed that he kept recurring to his "authors of the concrete"—Aristotle, Goethe, Kant, Kafka. He could convey a good deal about his view of life by simply mentioning the thinkers he had learned from, and he lists a dozen or so. "As I now think of all of them," he says, "and scores of other great authors, what stands out is the common enterprise: how to explain (or explain away) the matter-of-fact, the erotic, the abiding, and the unknown." He thought of himself on the same quest, "How it is and what to do."

The essay "Politics Within Limits" recapitulated much of what Goodman had said in his "Notes of a Neolithic Conservative," but as he became increasingly disengaged from the fray, his thoughts grew more philosophic. It was as if he were sketching out the book on ethics he had always wanted to write, touching on most of the issues raised in his social criticism but omitting the current events he typically used for ammunition. As a result, these political aphorisms have not dated with the passage of time, though readers familiar with *Growing Up Absurd* and *People or Personnel* will recall their origins. Here is his summary of "this politics of mine": it is

> the consistent package of conservative biases, the ideology of a peasant or a small entrepreneur who carries his office and capital under his hat. Localism, ruralism, face-to-face organization, distrust of planning, clinging to property, natural rights, historical privileges and immunities, letters to the editor that view with

18

alarm, carrying on the family craft, piecemeal reforms, make do, and let me alone.

...Since as experience I want the concrete and finite, with structure and tendency, a Next so I can live on a little, and a dark surrounding, politically I want only that the children have bright eyes, the river be clean, food and sex be available, and nobody be pushed around.

It would be possible to build an entire anarchist program from this essay, but Goodman's "Politics Within Limits" differs from his other social criticism in its personal slant. This is what *he* needed in order to get on with the real business of life. And so, on second thought, he decided that the deepest source of his values was his own childhood experience, "not a possessive peasant nor a threatened small entrepreneur, but a small child who needs the security of routine. There is no father. Mother is away all day at work. He is self-reliant because he has to be. It is lonely, but nobody bugs him, and the sun is pouring through the window."

Goodman liked to praise old-fashioned virtues, as he called them—prudence and temperance, frugality, honesty, forthrightness, generosity, magnanimity—the list was a combination of Aristotle's *Ethics* and the Boy Scout Handbook. In "Finite Experience" he singled out two "theological virtues" that he had first taken to heart as *his* particular bulwarks when he wrote his book on Kafka, who also relied on them. These were patience and fortitude, the bedrock of faith: "though I have faith that there is a world for me, I am foreign in it, I cannot communicate my needs, I do not share the customs, I am inept. So it is like a new world, I am as if resurrected, when the world is practicable. Therefore, until that moment, I put a premium on patience and fortitude." Although he sometimes spoke as if patience and fortitude were merely defenses against depriva-tion, at the cold end of the ethical spectrum, Goodman had a Taoist belief in them as positive virtues.

"Patience is drawing on underlying forces; it is powerfully positive, though to a natural view it looks like just sitting it out. How would I persist against positive eroding forces if I were not drawing on invisible forces?...

"Fortitude is to persist in one's task with an extra ounce of strength, after one has exhausted one's resources. As we say it in American, fortitude is to stay in there pitching. As I recall how often I have done it in bleak ball games and I have seen others do it, I realize it is a mystery."

Goodman had a third axiom to go with patience and forti-tude, though it had no traditional name or place in theology. This was what he called "going about your business," by which he meant that one was not simply to sit and sulk if the world seemed bleak or desperate; on the contrary, there was always something to do, namely to persist in what were evidently one's proper tasks, however life might have determined them. For him that meant writing poems and stories. In any case it would be something concrete, part of finite experience, one might say occupational therapy of the sort that keeps in the forefront the simple practicability of the world. Danger always lay in ab-straction, losing touch.

In Goodman's great comic epic *The Empire City* (1959) he had portrayed this third axiom as a special resource of women, whose lives were more likely to teach the efficacy of doing what is necessary. One of his female characters enunciates the prin-ciple: "Heavens! You men, with your irresistible forces and your immovable objects. So strenuous. . . . [W]hat to do? what to do? Go about your business, that's what to do." The hero echoes her: "It is always some concrete particular problem or other; and once I consider it this way, the solution, what to do, is always simple."

In "Finite Experience" Goodman explains why these three axioms of reliance on the nature of things were so important in his life. There was a kind of hope—"imagining, wishing, expecting"—which was the opposite or absence of concrete, practical life, "an abstraction not in touch with the real situation" and in his case "an utter curse." Although he speaks of it here in very general terms as "heated vision," "fantasy," "expecting the impossible," Goodman knew only too well that he was talking about his compulsive pursuit of sexual love. He also understood that this "crazy hope" expressed a deeper, archaic hunger in him, some fatal loss that could never be repaired, and made his lust insatiable. He called his fantasy of fulfillment "paradise"—chiefly to say that he was *not* in paradise, that paradise was lost, however much he had his heart set on it. Because his eros carried this great burden, he could not easily get in contact with any actual object of lust. Even success was likely to fall short of such wild hopes.

"Most often when I am hopeful, nothing at all eventuates. If something does happen to eventuate, I am overwrought and act foolishly.

"I do better, and suffer less, if I act with nonattachment, doing what is technically correct, expecting nothing; or acting generously, casting bread on the waters, expecting nothing. And if anything eventuates, if I cope with it like a present fact rather than the fulfillment of a wish."

That is, his task was to have patience and fortitude and to go about his business.

Goodman's paradisal hope was the other side of his contentment with the measure of ground under his feet, the finite experience and concrete reality so much of his book celebrates. A pragmatist such as he, apparently, was terribly susceptible to Platonic temptations: "Since we have no values except in the tendency of what we are doing, we cannot make a plan of action to a far goal; we have no goal, just the reality that we are dissatisfied. Then except by the miracle that events happen to converge in my poor Here Now and Next, the world is impracticable."

By devoting so much of his life to longing for paradise, Goodman had made his world into a desert with only two alternatives, mirage or miracle. It was not even that he wanted to achieve his actual goal. There could be no satisfying this longing for the ideal in the finite world of bodies and acts. He understood this, and many years earlier had admitted in his diary that the constant hunt for sexual love, cruising the streets so many afternoons for twenty-five years, must be a "cultus-religion," a false and empty obsession. He had finally worked himself free of it, at least insofar as the compulsive cruising was concerned, at about the time he became a famous man whose time was swallowed up by public duties; but the longing for some miraculous erotic visitation did not go away. Now in his essay on the religious dimensions of "Finite Experience" he faced it squarely. "I have despaired beforehand that my wish is what I want, and therefore I do not go about it practically to succeed. Yes, for the crazy glow of my hope, not its substance, is the color of what I really want, which is not possibly in the offing. And the horrible sinking of my disappointment is not for what I wished for, but because I am again reminded that I am not in paradise."

One of the ways Goodman coped with his crazy hope was through his art. Quite literally, when the object of desire failed to keep the appointment and Goodman was left alone in the bar nursing his beer, he invariably wrote another poem about

> The hours I've spent waiting at a place
> where somebody isn't coming there today
> until too late. . . .

But of course it was more than that. If Goodman cruised the streets most days, he also wrote every day, and his creative work was "imagining, wishing, expecting" in a realm somewhere between the concrete and the abstract, and closely related to the "play" of children. As he said in his "Apology for Literature," "There is no other discourse but literature that is subjective and objective, general and concrete, spontaneous and deliberate." He went on to explain its special use for him. "Literature confounds the personal and the impersonal, meaning and beginning to act, and thought and feeling. In this confusion which is like actual experience, it makes a kind of sense. It imagines what might be, taking account of what is. . . . It provides a friendly community across the ages and boundaries, and cheers my solitude. It is the way I pray to God." Goodman loved his art because it gave him respite from the dilemma of finite experience and crazy hope. It did not matter so much whether he was writing fiction and poems based on his own experience and desire or utopian sociology, like the books and essays he wrote during the sixties in which his aim was to escape the feeling of being trapped in things as they are—"they rescue me from the horror of metaphysical necessity, and I hope they are useful for my readers in the same way."

He tied his literary disposition quite explicitly to the need for a bridge between his longing for paradise and the practicable world. "I cannot take my wishes, feelings, and needs for granted and directly try to act them, as many other people seem to be able to do. I have to try to make sense, that is, to say my feelings and needs to myself and to other people. It is no doubt the sign of a deep anxiety....I have that kind of personality that first says and then initiates what it wants, and then knows what it wants, and then wants it....I tentatively say 'I love you' and find that I love you."

If Goodman wrote to find out what he wanted, to make desire practical, what are we to say of his parting words written at the end of his life, when he knew he was dying and there would soon be an end to both desire and practicality?

"How would I know?" I can hear him answering. "I gather together my finite experience that is scattering in confusion. Here it all is, like an offering. Thus I disown my experience and again come face to face with nothing."

He wrote these sentences on the recto of a page near the end; on the verso lay a poem.

I ask the Lord, "Who are You?"
though I know His name is "Spoken to."
Hoping but I am not sure
His name might be "I am who answer."

With certain faith let me continue
my dialogue with Spoken-To.
    Hope has always been my curse,
    it never yet came to pass.

The crazy man that you meet
talking to himself on the street
    is I, please gently lead him home.
    Creator Spirit come.

1

Within My Horizon

Some happy folk their faith
and some their calling doth
    justify, but Lord,
    I am justified

by the beauty of
the world and my love
    of your animals, though I
    haven't been happy thereby.

I CAN'T THINK ABSTRACTLY. Like everybody, I suppose—how would I know?—I start from concrete experience, but I have to stick to it. "Force" or "cause" always finally means to me that I give a push, or make it out of wood like a carpenter. Failing this, I cultivate my acre like a dumb peasant, and it grows maybe in spite of my efforts. I feel with Faraday when he said, "I never could know a fact that I didn't see"—he didn't mean that he was empirical, for all science is empirical, but that, the son of a blacksmith, he had to devise apparatus and produce the fact. As a writer, I almost never have a further purpose than just saying it; the structure that I find or put in the words is *universale in re*.

In these notes, paying attention to what I do, "bracketing it off" as Husserl says, I am spelling out where this leads me and how it traps me. It is both happy and unhappy.

I am faintly disgusted by ideas, *universale ante rem*. I had a Platonic spell as an adolescent, and my guess is that it is masturbating with an image that is distasteful, rather than just with my body. Or ideas are a surfeit, I can't keep them down.

I get lost, quickly confused, when people reason from classes of things, *universale post rem*. I usually dislike what they come out with because it is frigid and irrelevant. When I do admire abstract formal thinking, like mathematics, I take it like music, concrete after all. But then I am baffled how it can apply to anything beyond itself, as it seems to.

Let me give an example. In Western calisthenics we characteristically aim at an abstract standard of health and performance and devise exercises toward it; for the vital functions, we do chest-expansion and tone the heart, and we do push-ups and pull-ups for strength. In Prussian military exercises the goal is further predetermined, to create a martial attitude, pelvis retracted, chest up, chin in.

Chinese *tai-chi*, so far as I understand it, tries to activate every possible muscle by the flowing passage from posture to posture. So it is less predetermined by an abstract standard or extrinsic goal; it is tailored to the natural species. But it is not tailored to me, where and how I am.

The right exercises use the available powers that I have—limited by my tensions, inhibitions, illness, inattentiveness, disuse—and try to develop them, by the smallest increment possible, to what I don't do but could do. As the case is with me, the best next motion is often to relax. The art of the trainer is to notice what my body "wants" to do, and to suggest the appropriate posture and movement. The theory is that my organism tends to actualize itself if I stand out of the way. It is an article of faith.

The appropriate motion may be passionate: shouting at someone, weeping, or recoiling in fear. It may be intellectual: brow becoming perplexed; loosening watchful teeth, eyes, and breathing and becoming confused; or saying a complete sentence how I am. It may be "physical": throwing a punch or hauling water.

30

There are no right exercises without an object in the environment, though I may not yet know what it is.

Environment is not the roundabout space but the place *of*. It is the eco-niche in which only one species lives and reproduces, though it seems to be crowded with too many other species. The *amate* tree that I used to lie under in Cuernavaca was a whole aviary of ethnic neighborhoods at different levels and shadows. Conversely, there are big areas that are empty and undeveloped, but I doubt that they are underdeveloped.

It is the place of me now. It is not the climate that counts, nor even the day's weather; but that it was hot in the field leeward of the hill, to be playing a competitive game in which my relations with the others were too thick. I ought to have worn a hat. I did not chew my breakfast because of my bad teeth, and anyway my diet was deficient in vitamin E.—After I had the heart attack, the doctor forbade me to go swimming in the river, saying, "Of course, it's the ideal exercise for your condition, but there might always be a sudden emergency. Also, no driving for two months." Wise advice: be prudent. Quite impossible to follow, for it is the essence of the sudden that it happens all of a sudden, imprudently. Trying to avoid the sudden I can work myself into a state all of a sudden.

Goethe's contrary advice was probably wiser: "We commit some folly just to live on a little." But which? when? He—evidently!—knew the answer—as it turned out. The proof of a sage is that he lasts.

Experience is prior to the "organism" and the "environment," which are abstractions from experience. It is prior to "I" and "that there," which are abstractions. They are plausible, perhaps inevitable abstractions, except for moments of deep

31

absorption. They are said by every natural language, and it is the devil to try to invent a phenomenological language that avoids them. But we must be careful not to forget the matrix from which they are abstracted. There is no function of an organism that does not essentially involve its environment—we breathe air and walk by gravity and ground. No feeling that does not address the environment—anger that there is an obstacle to reaching, or an insult to organic integrity; grief that there is a hole in the environment, or a loss there that must be mourned through. If emotions did not signal something about the environment, they would not have been inherited and have survived; they tell the relation of organism and environment, and they spur us to cope.

Conversely, the actual environment, the place, is what is selected, structured, and appropriated by the organism.

Aristotle put it well: When the sensory power is actualized, when there *is* experience, the sense organ is the *same as* the sensed object. "The object of sight is the oval of vision."

Experience is neither "subjective" nor "objective." Its proper nouns are Here, Now, Next, Thou, We, rather than I, It, Past, Future. It is impossible to talk such language, but it is the genius of literature to recapture primary experience by combining narrator and narrative in ongoing plot. A man of letters will at any moment become personal in his essay; a sociologist may not.

Ideally, the operational style in science should recapture primary experience, but it invariably lacks courage and does not really bring in the investigator as an animal and person; instead, his operations themselves are described as objects. On the other hand, those who write the sociology or psychology of science usually, though not invariably, avoid the adventure and the objective discoveries in the field, the things that make it worthwhile to talk about scientists altogether. Instead, they become politically polemical or they psychoanalyze, introducing further abstractions. It is not interesting that Newton was mad unless we show how the inverse-square law of gravity is mad — which it perhaps is; and to the extent that the law of gravity was not altogether mad, we should revise our notions of what a madman is — we certainly should.

In my experience, experience occurs in finite but good-sized chunks. Each chunk roughly hangs together internally, but I have never experienced that All is One or that everything is connected. I have also never had a conversion or "blinding flash of insight," but very frequent insights, connections new to me, that I greet with a beck of the head saying "Hm," but rarely "Aha!" or "Wow!" When I have an insight, the rough structure is sharper or more vivid, rarely new.

The structure of experience is clearer if I pay attention without staring. If I can scan and meditate. I don't know — I have never really tried it — if there is a method, like the scientific method, that works to produce insight. Many of the fruits attributed to method are just a style of reporting what was already seen without the method. I myself usually pay attention after I have had an insight rather than to produce one, for it is easier to attend to what is interesting, what is becoming interesting.

Except when I am in pain or ill, my chunks of experience are quite sizable and complex, not small details or poor. There is plenty of room in them for me. (But because of chronic ailments I have suffered a lot of pain, and then my experience is constricted and boring.) I have never felt the wish to expand my consciousness, whether by drugs or political movements, or by identifying with the new generation—I just envy their vigor and sex. Indeed, I have found it hard to cope with the amount of consciousness I have.

My finite sizable chunks of experience are probably the same as the "normal" response to Rorschach cards: rarely seeing a Whole, rarely restricted to Small Details. In fact, however, my own Rorschach readings are inauthentic; I either see the cards too esthetically, as patches of shade and color and white space, or I see them too matter-of-factly as reproductions of inkblots. So in the theater I notice made-up actors, painted scenery, and artful speeches; I do not experience a theatrical illusion. I am sure I am missing something, but thereby, in my opinion, I better do get to know the playwright or whoever has been managing these things.

"Surrounding" finite experience must be what is not experienced. (This is an article of faith.) What, if anything, can be said about it from what is actual in experience?

In awareness there is a boundary of which one is still dimly aware, Husserl's "horizon"; and let us consider this in two different ways. First, if I turn to *it*, then what is beyond the boundary enters awareness. Whichever way I move, comes into being new space. To attend to the boundary is a standard device of psychotherapy: if there is an absence of feeling, trace the boundary of what *is* felt, for example, the air in the nostrils; then how far can you feel beyond the previous boundary, for example, air in the sinuses. Awareness itself seems to generate energy. They tell me there is a neurophysiological basis for this effect.

But the contrary tack is even more remarkable. If I withdraw further from the boundary by concentrating on the center, then the emptier the background is, the brighter and more structured the figure in the foreground. I take it that this is the idea of Yoga concentration. For my own theoretical purposes, I feign the hypothesis that energy flows from the emptying background and vivifies the figure in the foreground. I rely, by an act of faith, precisely on what I do not experience. Tao says, "Stand out of the Way." The implication is that there is then *new* energy, and theoretically, I like to deny the conservation of energy. But perhaps it is energy that we have dammed up and now set free, the tack that Horatio takes in *The Empire City*: "Let go, and it will move."

If in either case, attending to the boundary or withdrawing from it, the void is fertile, then it is very well that experience is finite.

Assume, as Berkeley pointed out about the oval of vision, that in general the field of experience is constant in size. Then, as we exclude what we do not intend to notice, the object of notice looms larger, nearer. It would take us over, except that I become dizzy. When I recover, I have lost the object and am having a different experience of constant size. This is Yang and Yin. Like the spaceman in *The Empire City*, I fail to experience the moment when *that* world which I am approaching becomes *this* world into which I have fallen.

I like a scientific explanation that is solidly grounded in what we do not know, for instance *The Origin of Species*. Darwin starts with varieties, from which he builds everything, and he knows nothing at all about the nature of variation. He did not know Mendel's laws of inheritance, nor chromosomes and genes, nor the causes of mutation. What is astounding is that he knew he did not know, instead of inventing some nonsense. But it is as if his ignorance let him really scrutinize the varieties, in domestication, in geographical distribution, in geological sequence. They were the matter, the material cause, dark but potential for *his* investigation. So Harvey had no way of connecting arteries and veins, but the blood circulated anyway.

There is an essential ignorance that clouds experience and prevents a good figure from forming in it; this gives me a headache until I find the missing clue; for instance, if the plot of a story doesn't work itself out because I have neglected something in the characters. But there is an essential ignorance in which I float happily, and that even seems to brighten what I do know, by contrast.

Put it the opposite way. To explain something in experience, we may pursue a chain of causes exploring back and back into what we do not know. But then the cause we arrive at will be abstract, and reduce the present concrete experience to what follows from other investigations, prior causes. It does not explain enough in the present experience. I prefer an explanation that saves the present experience as it is and copes with the problems that *it* poses, and tells me what it's made of, how it happens, how it works, how it hangs together, how to make it, where it's tending. Such explanations are themselves likely to raise questions and ask for other explanations, but then that will be a different concrete experience.

Pursuing a chain of causes, we may find necessary causes. But sufficient causes must be found in the concrete present.

To explain the negative, a failure, an illness, the lack of a necessary cause, we can draw on an abstraction. Kurt Goldstein used to point out that an injury to the optic nerve might prevent seeing; but one does not see with the optic nerve, nor with the eye, but with the whole organism, when there is light, and

36

so forth. So Hughlings Jackson: "One cannot explain a positive effect [an actual symptom] by a negative cause." By psychoanalysis of a childhood fixation, Freud explained why Leonardo did not paint more; he did not pretend to explain why he painted. The medievals said, *Natura sanat non medicus*: a physician may remove a source of infection or supplement a vitamin deficiency, but it is not he who restores function.

Unlike mathematicians, scientists may not reason by listing the possibilities and eliminating all but one. For the unknown may contain another possibility of explanation. It is likely to, or somebody would have reasoned it out long ago. Science must start from a fact. Aristotle: "Dialecticians reason from concepts; a scientist syllogizes from real premises."

Besides a rough structure, an intrinsic meaning, finite experience is usually ongoing and has a direction, an intrinsic end-in-view. So it has value. It wants to realize itself, practically or theoretically.

Since primary experience is prior to the distinction between subjective and objective, it is not yet a question whether the value is in the object or is felt into it by me. I myself do not remember any "value-free" experiences—perhaps one does not notice such. When an experience is consummatory, has no tendency either to fulfill itself or to try not to be, it is all the more value-laden, beautiful or tranquil, dismaying or despairing: "Stay!" or "I wish I were dead." For philosophers like Aristotle or Spinoza, the value of an achieved truth was happiness itself, the mind in action, or *hilaritas*, God's joy.

It is discouraging that recently scientists want to say that science is value-neutral, while indeed they are practicing beautiful personal and social virtues: honesty, accuracy, adventurousness, perseverance, humility, statement in due form, concern for public replication. Their science is rich with these virtues as well as truth, elegance, and possible utility. It must be that they have lost their heroic *élan* and are on the defensive. I think they are frightened by the inevitable abuse of the forces they unleash, so they hasten to disown responsibility, rather than trying politically to prevent the abuse, which is all any of us can do. (I do not think a scientist, or anybody else, has the option *not* to do his thing.)

The nature of things is wonderfully amenable to the heroic virtues of science. One can easily conceive a universe that does not reward patient effort, or where no setup is publicly replicable; but as Einstein put it, "God is subtile but not mean"—He does not deceive, the evidence is not planted to mislead us. God is hard to scrutinize but (to Einstein) He is not inscrutable. William Bateson used to urge his students to "cherish your exceptions," just as the Good Shepherd leaves the flock to rescue the lamb who has gone astray.

To bypass the problems of psychophysical interactions, Russell postulated that they happened in a "neutral stuff"; but this formulation comes to the same thing as saying "incarnate spirit," and it is as ideological. It is interesting that Russell used such self-denying language about reality when elsewhere he speaks so passionately about the erotic drive of his active intellect; it is as if he will never get what he loves because she's a cold fish. His friend Whitehead more complacently saw Deity emerging from matter like Aphrodite from the foam.

The naturalist school of novelists have also cultivated the notion that the facts are value-neutral, but by their treatment they disown the facts and are transparently saying, "Damn them." These same value-neutral facts happen to build into the writer's *summum bonum*, developing and climactic plot, tragedy.

Among academics, insistence on the value-neutral feels like chronic low-grade spite. It used to be the custom, from Aristotle until quite recent times, to introduce a course of lectures with a panegyric on the subject, its utility, or how ennobling to study it just for itself. Nowadays, in my observation, professors seem resentfully to disown what they are teaching. Indeed, among the younger radical sociologists of knowledge, the disposition is to show that a disinterested scholar, who values just what he is doing, is a witting or unwitting agent of the Central Intelligence Agency. At least this is not value-neutral.

To sum up, I stick pretty close to the concrete and finite, that comes in sizable chunks with a rough structure and an ongoing tendency and is immersed in ignorance, a void that is sometimes fertile. Such experience is roomy enough for me, usually meaningful, and sometimes valuable. And I have priggishly been pointing out its advantages.

Put in a different light, I am stuck with a poor way of being and thinking. Since I can't, or won't, readily think abstractly or symbolically, I can't get out of the stream when it would be useful to do so. Let me try to say it accurately. I am not drowning; I am not like an aphasic who cannot conceptualize his experience and so is vulnerable to "catastrophic reactions" (Kurt Goldstein); I conceptualize very well. I am only occasionally swamped and burst into tears. But I do not have moments of free choice. I probably do not know what freedom feels like. I will soon discuss my anarchism—I do not ground it in freedom. (Is it unconsciously a lust for freedom from my own tyranny, my *will* to be concrete and finite and make sense?)

My choices have been unusually autonomous, originating from myself, but—as I compare myself to some people—*I* never made them, and I never *made* them. I did not choose to be a writer, to live with my wives, to teach in schools, to be a Dutch uncle to the young, and so forth. Rather, I drifted into these because they were what I could do with my available means and opportunities, or was asked to do in actual situations when there seemed to me to be no other alternatives, or they were where my desires landed me though it was not what I wanted. These landing places then worked out and persisted because I could farm them well, and they chose me. I don't complain that I have been forced into anything. On the contrary, I am canny and stubborn, except for a short spell, in resisting and rejecting what doesn't suit, what doesn't have some kind of sense, what violates my honor and integrity. I can resist what is incompatible with my concrete experience, but I have no perspective to choose something else.

Goethe's advice to the youth was good, "Do what you can, not what you want," for the youth was alienated, a product of Sturm und Drang, and needed a material connection with the world. It is not good advice for me.

My inability to stand outside the stream of the concrete, watch it, and freely choose, is especially disastrous when I am bogged down in compulsive repetitions that don't work. Surely it would often be better for me to make an abstract judgment of what I want and where I am, to will a clear-cut decision, and to use purely instrumental means to succeed. Rather than to persist like Oblomov in Goncharov's book.

But for some reason I feel it is wicked to use a calculated means to get what I want, for instance to end up in bed with some one, though I do *not* disapprove what I want. I will not use such means, and I do not get what I want.

I do not disapprove my vices, but I disapprove a calculated plan to succeed in satisfying them. As I will say it later, happiness must happen, be a proof that we live in paradise, or why bother?

Yet the concrete is at least real, even if really lousy. The abstract wish is usually delusory, and the calculated means don't work anyway. Goethe again, "Beware what you wish for in your youth, for you will end up getting it in your middle age."

A married couple torment each other; if they break up, they will probably be happier, and surely be healthier, at least for a time. Yet they might not then have any one important in their lives, and is empty happiness worth it? The decision to break up is probably correct only if they are in fact involved elsewhere. Like science, personal relations must start from facts, not possibilities.

Since they are not organized by abstract concepts, my finite chunks of experience often do not add up; but I regard this rather complacently. I am usually consistent enough without having to be systematic. My Father's house has many mansions, and personally I am not very ambitious; I work hard to improve each shining hour, but I don't much care if I get anywhere. I don't hanker after any overwhelming climax of experience, a surpassing orgasm, or an expansion of consciousness.

But it is another matter when various chunks of experience do jar badly or are in outright conflict; or when drifting on one, I find myself on the shoals for the next. Each chunk of life has its intrinsic and therefore justified value, but I have no standard to make them commensurate, and little system to organize

41

them practically. I am not referring especially to basic "tragic" conflicts, between absolute values like compassion and truth, honor and loyalty, love and duty, in which I am sometimes trapped like any other serious person; but just the embarrassments that afflict a man who is busy, desirous, and disorganized. Suddenly I must cope with too many commitments, interests that are contradictory.

My pathetic expedient is to affirm both sides of the contradiction and carry on, not even hoping that something will turn up to extricate me, but just because I am at a loss what else to do, and I proceed by routine. In serious tragic conflicts, such a loyalty to contradictory absolute values is *chosen* and it has grandeur; it deserves the *deus ex machina* who saves the hero in some Greek plays; and maybe it is better to die than to betray an absolute though finite good. But in ordinary hang-ups like mine, I anxiously act out each side more strenuously than is necessary; I get no satisfaction on either side; there is not enough time for anything and there is still more miscalculation; friction increases. Till finally I am so weary that I have to withdraw from the field and lose both parties, and I have a host of psychosomatic symptoms to preoccupy me instead.

They say that it feels good to stop beating your head against a wall, but a person like that immediately develops other aches and pains.

But it's not so bad as that; I am omitting one factor, art, that is always either present in my experience or very near. It has made the difference, I think, between my life being wretched or just unhappy.

In a novel *Making Do* I draw the older man, one of the two protagonists, quite literally from myself, except that I explicitly

42

will not let him be an artist in his distress and fortitude; he can't have this out. I do have it.

Though I cannot will much for myself, I have a strong will to shape. If something goes well, I finish off by praising it. If it goes badly, I make something of it anyway by saying it. And the *products* of art add up; they join thousands of years of human culture around the world, bringing me into a great company. What could have been a fragmented existence has become a regular and respected career. (To be sure, if I hadn't had the disposition of an artist, I would have had some other disposition.)

— I am driving to the University around Koko the old volcano, to give a lecture that is not useful, nor do I much care if the students learn anything. I don't believe in modern universities. I am here to spend the winter in Hawaii and I have to have some occupation and excuse for being here. There are so many young fellows at the University, maybe I can find a lover for my loneliness. Suddenly, arching the highway is a great Hawaiian rainbow, the "gentle shock of mild surprise" that unlooses a poem. One foot of the rainbow is planted in Manoa Valley on the campus. And the point of the poem is that I will not find a pot of gold there, nor will I bring one. It turns out to be a good little poem. — I certainly do not have experiences in order to write poems about them. But what I experience is certainly congenial to the poems that I will write.

It is a hard question if art-will is *my* will. The urgency to write a poem rather comes to me; I cannot neglect it without bad consequences, boredom, distraction, insomnia. The subject, the "first line," usually chooses itself and often says itself; it is what I have noticed in a peculiar way, not my way — Wordsworth analyzes it well. The arc of the whole, as a beginning, middle, and end, is not planned, though I steer it and as a critic after the fact I can demonstrate it if anybody wants to know. The product, and having produced it, does nothing for me in the way of making me happier or wiser—it is a typical repetitive act springing, as Freud said, instead of a symptom. (Of course a symptom is itself an artistic act.) Admiring readers have not gone out of their way to give me what I need.

In other senses, it is my poem. I am absorbed and happy while making it, that is, I do not notice how I am. I ride with its process. It is in my style and domesticates experience for me. It forms my further style, so that finally I experience what I can write. (I have learned to write in a style that allows me to experience a good deal.) I am proud of the product and I want fame for it and me.

For both better and worse, my writing is colored with the bias of the rest of my experience, toward the concrete, intrinsic, literal, and finite. Allegory makes me squeamish. The use of "symbols" seems to me to be sophomoric. Poetry with a moral or political purpose sets my teeth on edge. "Poetry" itself must not be an abstraction, a genre. The basis of poetic diction is good colloquial speech, and I do not intone my poems but read them for their prose sense. What moves me most is just saying the sentences and paragraphs, the motion and progress of meanings. The big pattern of motion—long and short passages, slow and quick passages—is the chief organization of many of my stories. The propositional truth of the sentences, their correspondence to reality, is indifferent to me, though I prefer not to be trivial or stupid. The possible effect on the readers never crosses my mind. (I do not care about them and they, catching the signal, give nothing to me while I age and die.)

44

The term "abstract art" has unfortunately gotten to be applied to precisely the most intrinsic and concrete art, the acting of the artist in the medium. "Abstract art" was so called because it dispensed with an external model; but when I here say that I do not "abstract," "abstraction" means generalization or class name, or external standard (including fidelity to a model), as opposed to intrinsic end-in-view. Words are about situations, but men of letters act literarily, concretely, they *tell* the situations.

Preparing a play, if an actress bogs down on certain lines, I strike them. I compose a speech that she can say well. I write in a new part for an actor because he looks like that. There are special architectural features to the stage — it is a church — so I remake the climactic scene in order to use them. It is better that the play has ringing voices and a grip on material reality than to try to say what I used to intend. Somebody can play the flute; why not a song for the flute, that beautiful instrument? Aristotle said, "Only the flute has the song of the flute," meaning that the matter, wood, is intrinsic to its form, the melody. Oddly, we still put our silver flutes among the woodwinds.

And it has its bad side. Since I stick so closely to concrete experience, I cannot really write fiction. I am uneasy if I replace the name of my lover in a poem by a made-up metrical equivalent, and art is hurt by fetishism. I can fantasize only my own dreams; in 1950 I dreamed of flying, so in *The Dead of Spring* they fly. I cannot act a character on the stage, I turn into wood without a melody. Even in delivering a lecture, I either just carry on a conversation with members of the audience, or I just think aloud for the audience, for I can be myself without embarrassment. The only psychoanalytic paper on writing that I ever wrote is on this theme: the inability to imagine fictions, sticking too closely to the actuality. I interpreted it to mean that there is something in the actuality that is repressed and *not* said, that pins the imagination.

I will try to make a balance. My literalness is a clog to flights of imagination, but it saves me from frigid fancies. It keeps me from standing apart and getting a view of what is, but by nagging just how it is I often find meanings that I didn't know I knew. And I do well what I do.

> —I have among the Americans
> the gift of earnest speech
>   that says how a thing is.
>   If I do not, who will do it?

> —Austere is the praise
> that I have learned to sing
>   in verses out of my life
>   as burgeons the spring.

2

Politics
Within Limits

If I undertake to say
the conscience of my country,
    I only do my duty.
    But, Lord, it was not I

who chose it, but the hungry heart
and level look that you allotted
    to me when you did burden
    with different gifts different men.

THERE IS AN ODD ABSTRACTION "Society," that has exercised a superstitious compulsion on political scientists since the time of Bentham, Comte, Hegel, and Marx; instead of the loose matrix of face-to-face communities, private fantasies, and shifting subsocieties in which most people mostly live their lives. It is understandable that fatherly czars or divine-right monarchs would have the delusion that all the sparrows are constantly under their tutelage as Society; and that Manchester economists would sternly rule out of existence all family, local, and non-cash transactions that cannot be summed up on the Stock Exchange. The usual strategy of Enlightenment philosophers, however, was to cut such big fictions down to size and to have simple real abuses to reform. But after the French Revolution, it was as if, to substitute for the slogan L'Ancien Régime, it was necessary to have a concept equally grand, Society.

Comte and Bentham wanted to make the big fiction of Society for real— Comte knew that it started as a fiction— in order to use it to tidy up "everything" or at least "the greatest good for the greatest number." For metaphysical reasons, Hegel was satisfied that the more socialized a man, and the more self-conscious of it, the more real he was. But the pathetic case is Marx, who concentrated on Society and indeed wanted to empower Society, precisely to get rid of it and go back to simpler personal and community existence.

Certainly there are occasions when my existence as a mere member of Society is overwhelmingly important and not at all an abstraction, for example when they herd me onto a big airliner, with its backup of thousands of anonymous operatives and their schedules and instruments. But even so, after the initial shock, I soon recover and become restive for a more attractive seat-mate, or look for a couple of empties so I can stretch out and go to sleep, or I press my nose to the window and watch the clouds and the receding earth.

Usually my need for Society is satisfied by a very loose criterion: "Lucky is the man who can band together with enough of those like-minded with himself— it needs only a couple of hundred— to reassure him that he is sane, even though eight million others are quite batty" (*Empire City*, 1, 19, i).

By a good intuition, the best of the young dissidents disown abstract Society and want to be "just human." But they still reify it too much as the hostile "System," which exists but less than they think. Since they do not know concretely enough what they mean by "just human," they need a tangible adversary to give themselves shape. (But how, at my age, would I know what they mean?)

Most words of ordinary speech, of course, are simple abstractions, for classes of persons, things, relations, and so forth. Except in poetry and sociable chatter, the feel of the usual words is not Here, Now, Next— these are reduced to adverbs. Instrumental speech is likely to be abstract.

Simple abstractions need not be problematic. I can say, "There are our friends coming" and soon the words are "You— Here— Now— We— Next." But when there are difficulties— for instance, what if they are not our friends, and do not even speak our language and do not want to share our experience?— then we must resort to psychotherapy, politics, and pastoral theology to unmake alienation.

The critical question for me is how to have, or make, those abstractions "Organism," "Environment," "History," so that they can possibly interact to reconstitute primary experience. I have written ten books on this question in various contexts. "To have an environment and not take it as an object, is Tao," said Chuang-tzu. Sometimes I state my program in the form, "How to take on Culture without losing Nature," but that is already too abstract.

A conclusion I have reached is this: Like Luther, but unlike Hegel or Marx, I think that the way to overcome alienation is to go home and not on a tour through history and the realms of being. It is also true, however, that a man who is on the Way deviates and does not err.

In *Gestalt Therapy*, I reason my way into the subject as follows: If we envisage an animal moving, continually seeing new scenes and meeting new problems to cope with, it will continually have to make a creative adjustment. Selecting, initiating, shaping, in order to appropriate the novelty of the environment to itself, and to screen out what would destroy homeostasis. Adjusting, because the organism's every living power is actualized only in its environment. And the environment, for its part, must be amenable to appropriation and selection; it must be plastic to be changed and meaningful to be known. The precipice that you fall off is not your environment.

51

Aristotle says it succinctly, "Food is the unlike that can become like." Or, in a passage I have already quoted, "Perceiving is the identity of the object of sense and the activated sensory organ." — I like to quote Aristotle on these matters because he was the sophisticated climax of *prima facie* observations, and his formulations are drily pithy lecture notes. But I do not think his doctrine was different from Kant's, who was critical of two thousand years of philosophizing and came to the same *prima facie* observations, "The percept is blind, the concept is empty," "the synthetic unity of apperception," "judgment is not a categorical proposition."

Then I conclude, abnormal psychology is the therapy of disturbances of creative adjustment, for example, rigid or archaic responses.

And we can speak similarly of abnormal sociology: it is politics, to remedy institutions that hinder experience from occurring, for example, roles rather than vocations, individuals or collectives rather than people in communities, whatever prevents citizens from initiating and deciding, or makes it complicated for craftsmen and professionals to practice.

There is no politics but remedial politics; often the first remedy is to take "Society" less seriously, and to notice what society one has.

As I review my books of social criticism and my occasional trips in therapy and politics, I am pleased at how they flow temperamentally from my biases about experience. My kind of anarchism, pacifism, and decentralism; opposition to mandarinism and schooling; emphasis on vocation and profession; ecology and neighborhood in physical planning; rural reconstruction; intermediate technology for underdeveloped

52

regions; my "neolithic conservatism"—these are congenial to a bias for the concrete, finite, and artistic, *universale in re* and intrinsic end-in-view. Such as they are, my political ideas are authentic.—In fact, I haven't changed them since I was a boy, though there has been a lot of history since then. This must be partly because I don't learn anything, but it is partly because political truth is so simple that a boy can see it with a frank look, namely: Society with a big S can do very little for people except to be tolerable, so they can go on about the more important business of life.

It's an impressive list of topics that I spread myself thin over. To me, naturally, my opinions confirm one another by being coherent with one another wherever I look. The proof of a literary style is that it is viable over a wide range of experience, to say it.

A generalist is a man who knows something about many special sciences, in order to coordinate their conclusions in a system that has little relation to reality. A man of letters knows only a little about some major human concerns, but insists on relating what he does know to his concrete experience. So he explores reality. A generalist is interdisciplinary. A man of letters finds that the nature of things is not easily divided into disciplines.

My social ideas are temperamentally mine, but they do not derive logically from my biases, as a doctrine. I would abhor a politics, pedagogy, or town-planning deduced from metaphysics or epistemology, or even scientifically deduced, rather than being pragmatic and not immoral. One must not manipulate real people because of an idea or a confirmed hypothesis. Indeed, I say "not immoral" rather than "moral" because positive morality, when used as a principle for action, can be more abstract and imperial than anything. There are far too many missionaries among my friends.

But instead of being abstract or moral, my corresponding defect is that I am an artist and fundamentally unpolitical. I don't (timidly) bestir myself to oppose anything or try to change it unless I first have imagined a simpler and more artistic way to do it, neater, making use of available materials, less senseless, less wasteful. If a bad situation is not amenable to my flash of inventiveness, I find it hard to identify with it as mine; I feel there's nothing that I can contribute. Meantime people are suffering. But a political person ploughs into the situation and makes a difference in it just by his action. Sometimes a good idea then turns up.

Artistic visions have their virtues. (Let me speak no evil of the Creator Spirit.) They are better than carping criticism. They give people a ray of light instead of the gloom of metaphysical necessity. Activism and ideology both do more harm than good. But art has the unpolitical self-sufficiency of art. I am not zealous to make my models real. And they have the timidity of being personal; I draw no strength from my fellows; I cannot lead and find it hard to follow.

One cannot rely on artists for a political message. Tolstoy makes war seem sublime and attractive. Homer makes it senseless and horrible.

But I mustn't overstate my diffidence. I, like anybody else, see outrages that take me by the throat, and no question of not identifying with them as mine. Insults to the beauty of the world that keep me indignant. Lies, triviality, and vulgarity that suddenly make me sick. The powers-that-be do not know what it is to be magnanimous; often they are simply officious and spiteful. As Malatesta used to say, you try to live better and they intervene, and then *you* are to blame for the fight that happens. Worst of all, it is clear from their earth-destroying actions that these people are demented, sacrilegious, and will bring down doom on themselves and those associated with them; so sometimes I am superstitiously afraid to belong to the same tribe and walk the same ground as they.

Yet men have a right to be crazy, stupid, or arrogant. It is our specialty. Our mistake is to arm anybody with collective power. Anarchy is the only safe polity.

It is a moral disaster to suppress indignation, nausea, and scorn; it is a political (and soon moral) disaster to make them into a program. Their right political use is negative, to band together to stop something.

It is a common misconception that anarchists hold that "human nature is good" and therefore men can rule themselves. But we tend rather to be pessimistic. We are phlegmatic because we do not have ideas. And men in power are especially liable to be stupid because they are out of touch with concrete finite experience and instead keep interfering with other people's initiative, so they make them stupid too. Imagine being deified like Mao Tse-tung or Kim Il Sung, what that must do to a man's character. Or habitually thinking the unthinkable, like our Pentagon.

Most anarchist philosophers start from a lust for freedom. Sometimes this is a metaphysico-moral imperative, with missionary zeal attached, but mostly it is a deep animal cry or religious yearning, like the hymn of the prisoners in *Fidelio*. They have seen or suffered too much restraint—serfdom, factory slavery, deprived of liberties, colonized by an imperialist, befuddled by the church.

My experience, however, has by and large been roomy enough. "They" have not managed to constrict it too much, though I have suffered a few of the usual baits, many of the punishments, and very many of the threats. I do not need to shake off restraint in order to be myself. My usual gripe has been not that I am imprisoned, but that I am in exile or was born on the wrong planet. My real trouble is that the world is impractical for me; by impatience and cowardice I make it even less practical than it could be.

For me, the chief principle of anarchism is not freedom but autonomy, the ability to initiate a task and do it one's own way. Without orders from authorities who do not know the actual problem and the available means. External direction may sometimes be inevitable, as in emergencies, but it is at a cost to vitality. Behavior is more graceful, forceful, and discriminating without the intervention of the state, wardens, corporation executives, central planners, and university presidents. These tend to create a chronic emergency that makes them necessary. In most cases, the use of power to do a job is inefficient in the fairly short run. Extrinsic power inhibits intrinsic function. "Soul is self-moving," says Aristotle.

The weakness of "my" anarchism is that the lust for freedom is a powerful motive for political change, whereas autonomy is not. Autonomous people protect themselves stubbornly but by less strenuous means, including plenty of passive resistance.

The pathos of oppressed people, however, is that, if they break free, they don't know what to do. Not having been autonomous, they don't know what it's like, and before they learn, they have new managers who are not in a hurry to abdicate. The oppressed hope for too much from New Society, instead of being vigilant to live their lives. They had to rely on one another in the battle, but their solidarity becomes an abstraction and to deviate is called counterrevolutionary.

The possibility of my weaker position is that autonomous people might see that the present situation is disastrous for them, and that their autonomy is whittled away. They cannot help but see it. There is not enough useful work and it is hard to do it honestly or to practice a profession nobly. Arts and sciences are corrupted. Modest enterprise must be blown out of all proportion to survive. The young cannot find their vocations. Talent is stifled by credentials. Taxes are squandered on war, schoolteachers, and overhead. And so forth, and so on. The remedies for all this might be piecemeal and undramatic, but they must be fundamental, for many of the institutions cannot be recast and the system itself is impossible. A good deal could be made tolerable by wiping a good deal off the slate.

The aim of politics is to increase autonomy, and so it is mostly undoing. I like the Marxist formula "the withering away of the State," but it is the method, not the result.

The central organization of administration, production, and distribution is sometimes unavoidable, but it mathematically guarantees stupidity. Information reported from the field must be abstracted, and it loses content at every level; by the time it reaches headquarters it may say nothing relevant. Or it may say what (it is guessed) headquarters wants to hear. To have something to report, the facts of the field are molded into standard form and are no longer plastic. Those in headquarters cannot use their wits because they are not in touch. Those in the field lose their wits because they have to speak a foreign tongue, and can't initiate anything anyway. On the basis of the misinformation it receives, headquarters decides, and a directive is sent down that may fit nobody in particular. At each level it is enforced on those below in order to satisfy those above, rather than to do the work. When it is applied in the field, it may be quite irrelevant, or it may destroy the village in order to save it.

The criteria for the success of such operations are abstractions like Gross National Product, Standard of Living, body count, passenger-miles, Ph.D.'s awarded. These at best have no relation to the common wealth, satisfaction of life, peace, experience of travel, or knowing anything. But at worst they impede the common wealth, peace, experience of travel, and so forth.

Nevertheless, central organization, that mathematically guarantees stupidity, is sometimes unavoidable; and just by existing, it exerts disproportionate power. This is a puzzler. The Articles of Confederation and the acrimoniously debated Federalist Constitution gave an answer that worked pretty well, in quite simple conditions, for almost thirty years.

I suppose the most sickening aspect of modern highly organized societies is the prisons and insane asylums, vast enclaves of the indigestible, that the rest live vaguely aware of, with low-grade anxiety.

We have been getting rid of the stupid but at least human notions of punishment, revenge, "paying the debt," and so forth. But instead, there persists and grows the Godlike assumption of "correcting" and "rehabilitating" the deviant. There is no evidence that we know how; and in both prisons and asylums it comes to the same thing, trying to beat people into shape, treating the inmates like inferior animals, and finally just keeping the whole mess out of sight.

58

The only rational motive for confining any one is to protect ourselves from injury that is likely to be repeated. In insane asylums, more than 90 percent are harmless and need not be confined. And in prisons, what is the point of confining those—I don't know what percent, but it must be fairly large—who have committed one-time crimes, for example, most manslaughters and passional or family crimes, while they pay up or atone? People ought indeed to atone for the harm they have done, to get over their guilt and be "rehabilitated," but this is much more likely to occur by trying to accept them back into the community, rather than isolating and making them desperate. Certainly the old confession on the public square was a better idea.

It is doubtful that punishing some deters others. Varying the penalties has no statistical effect on occurrence, but only measures the degree of abstract social disapproval. And it is obvious that the great majority who do not steal, bribe, forge, and so forth, do not do so because of their life-style, more subtile influences than gross legal risks; other cultures, and some of our own subcultures, have other styles and other habits—for example, the youth counterculture has much increased shoplifting and forging of official documents.

The chief reason that so-called "moral legislation" has no influence in deterring vices is that temptation to the vices does not occur in the same psychological context as rational calculation of legal risks—unlike business fraud or risking a parking ticket. And it is likely that much authentic criminal behavior is compulsive in the same way.

There are inveterate lawbreakers and "psychopathic personalities" who cannot be trusted not to commit the same or worse crimes. (I think they will exist with any social institutions whatever.) It is unrealistic to expect other people not to panic because of them, and so we feel we have to confine them, instead of lynching them. But our present theory of "correction" in fact leads to 70 percent recidivism, usually for more serious felonies; to a state of war and terrorism between prisoners and guards; and to increasing prison riots. Why not say honestly, "We're locking you up simply because we're afraid of you. It is not necessarily a reflection on you and we're sorry for it. Therefore, in *your* terms, how can we make your confinement as painless and profitable to you as we can? We will give you as many creature satisfactions as you wish and we can afford, not lock you in cells, let you live in your own style, find and pursue your own work—so long as *we* are safe from you. A persisting, and perhaps insoluble, problem is how you will protect yourselves from one another."

It may be objected, of course, that many sober and hardworking citizens who aren't criminals are never given this much consideration by society. No, they aren't, and *that* is a pity.

Writing *Communitas*, my brother and I used only one methodical criterion: diminish intermediary services that are not directly productive or directly enjoyed, like commuting, packaging, sewer lines, blue books. These do not pay off as experience, but they clutter it up and rigidly predetermine it—you walk where the streets go. The social wealth and time of life that go into intermediaries cannot be used for something else. There are slums of engineering. Economists of the infrastructure do not think enough about this when they saddle underdeveloped regions with dead weight.

It is melancholy to consider the fate of John Dewey's instrumentalism, the idea that meaning and value are imbedded in means and operations, that the end-in-view is *in* practice. Instrumentalism was attacked as anti-intellectual, as base because it omitted ideals; but indeed it was an attempt to rescue intellect from being otiose and merely genteel. It was part of the same impulse as functionalism to rescue architecture, and industrial democracy and agrarian populism to rescue democracy. These meant to dignify the everyday and workaday from being servile means for Sunday goals. Now, however, we take it for granted that immense means are employed and operations carried on *instead* of meaning and value. No end-in-view, no experience, nothing practical. A university is administered to insure its smooth administration. The government makes work in order to diminish unemployment. A candidate runs for office in order to be elected. A war is fought to use new weapons. Only the last of these sounds harsh.

At best, survivals of the past, for example "Western culture," and the busy business of present society, must also be crushing weights on anybody's poor finite experience, unless he can somehow appropriate them as his own by education and vocation.

Most people in most ages pick up a good store of folkways and folk songs in the same way as they learn the language, however that is. They prudently manage to screen out most of the high thought and culture that is not for them, unless they are harassed by schoolteachers; yet they also get wonder-full flashes of it: on solemn religious occasions; from works of high music, art, and architecture that have become like folkways; from important civic occasions that give food for profound thought, like constitutional crises, struggles for social justice, law suits; and most jobs and crafts, whether mechanics or farming or cooking or child-rearing, involve a good deal of fundamental

61

science and high tradition that intelligent people pick up. Ordinary life can be culturally rich, and sometimes has been. It is a dubious society when the workdays, holidays, and election days do not provide enough spirit for most people, and we try to give a liberal education abstractly by lessons in school. It cannot be done.

In critical periods, alienated young people may choose on principle not to take on the traditions at all. At the end of the Middle Ages, the *moderni* declared they were throwing out the past and they deserted the Scholastic regent professors and set up their own colleges. The youth of Sturm und Drang threw out the courtly manners and morals. Today seems to be a similar time. Young people astoundingly may not know *Greensleeves* and *Annie Laurie*; they do not become thoughtful on days that commemorate events that happened thousands of years ago— like Huck Finn, they aren't interested in people who are dead; they take for granted what Harvey and Newton had to puzzle out; they don't care that Tyrannosaurus lorded it over the Cretaceous. The curriculum of a Free University might be, typ- ically, Sensitivity Training, Psychedelic Experience, Multi- Media, Astrology, Castro's Cuba, History of Women, and Black Studies. These are not the major humanities, yet it is better to study what they *can* appropriate as experience than what they can't. (I am puzzled that they do not study nothing, a deeply philosophical subject. They seem to have to go to school.)

Some of us, finally, live *in* the high culture, its spirit reviv- ing in us and being more or less relevant to 1972, not with an easy adjustment. Our contemporaries are as likely to be Seami and Calderón as people we can talk to. People like us have a use. It would be woeful if the great moments of spirit did not survive. And the present institutions are lifeless if their spirit is not revived. But I don't know any method to teach what we know, namely that Beethoven, the Reformers, the authors of *The Federalist*, were real people and meant what they did. The great difficulty is that, in order to know them in our terms, it is first necessary to make the abnegation of learning them in their terms. And the less culture one has to begin with, the harder this is to do.

Vocation is taking on the business of the community so it is not a drag. If I find what I am good at and good for, that my community can use and will support, securely doing this, I can find myself further; and the social work is humanized because a real person is really doing it.

Having a vocation is always somewhat of a miracle, like falling in love and it works out. I can understand why Luther said that a man is justified by his vocation, for it is already a proof of God's favor. Naturally, it is psychologically easier if the family or community has provided intimate models to a child, and if it encourages him as he follows his own bent. It is harder if a child is poor or is restricted by his status, high or low, and has to take what offers or what he must. Faraday's career is a good example of both advantage and deprivation, and of the miracle. His father was a journeyman blacksmith. When he was adolescent, they apprenticed him to a bookbinder for seven years. Although he could hardly read, he used to take home the books of natural philosophy that came into the shop for rebinding, and copy out the diagrams. The clients talked to him—he must have been likeable as well as smart. They invited him to lectures. Because of his ability to fashion apparatus, at twenty he became the laboratory assistant of Humphry Davy. So he had the right background, he had the right hardships to make him make an effort, and he had the genius of Faraday.

Our present practice is poor. Big Society has slots to fill; the young are tested for their aptitudes and schooled to fill the slots. There are no intimate models. The actual jobs are distant and unknown. Talent is co-opted; it does not develop at the youth's choice and time. A strong talent may well balk and deny his very talent. This is abstract.

But there may be an even more lifeless future, now widely proposed. The young must be trained to be adaptable to "play various roles." This will "free" people from being "tied down." Young people I have talked to like this idea; being "just human" means not limited to a vocation or profession. They want to be "into" various activities. As presumably Shakespeare was heavily into writing plays and Niels Bohr was into atomic physics. It is a curious view of personality and commitment.

To be a citizen is the common vocation. It is onerous unless one has an authentic talent for it, which I don't have, but we have to take over society as our (hopefully finite) experience or it takes us over infinitely. Even when I can only gripe, I write letters to the editor. I gave a collection of them the explanatory title *The Society I Live In Is Mine*.

A child or adolescent has the right to naïve patriotism, loyal pride in the place where he is thrown—he didn't choose to be born here. Without a sneaking nostalgia that there is *some* sense, honorable history, and good intentions in these people, we are in a harsh exile indeed.

For a child, even the idiot patriotism of nationalism is better than none. My little daughter, now nine, is going to an Hawaiian public school where they inundate the kids with

"Columbia the Gem of the Ocean" and the Pledge of Allegiance, plus some pathetic Hawaiiana—the school is 95 percent quarter-Polynesian. But in New York she had been attending a "progressive" private school where instead of "America the Beautiful" they were likely to sing,

> O ugly for polluted skies,
> grain grown with pesticides...

and I am just as pleased that (for a few months) she is reading about the shot heard round the world and Thomas Jefferson without mention of his being a slaveholder. I see that it makes her happier to believe the noble rather than the base. It is touching.

"I have no idea what is the secret mission of the Navy vessels lying off my lanai in Waimanalo, but I wish they would get it over with and stop obstructing the horizon."—letter to the *Honolulu Star-Bulletin*. In fact they were practicing living in an underwater habitat built by the Oceanic Institute, nothing objectionable. But my resentment was that the Navy just sat there day after day, as if they owned the place.

I like Hegel's idea that property is an extension of personality; it is obviously so if we consider my tools, my clothes, my room, and my view of the horizon. And I would prefer to consider big capital property in the same light rather than that it is made purely by statute, state power. But it is largely our common inheritance that has been sequestered by a few. Property has come to mean not facilitating use, but excluding others from use.

Socialists object to any theory of natural property. They would in fact usually allow private use in clothes, tools, and so forth, but not as a natural right, rather as a right given by the collective. I think this is dispiriting; in order to assert my right and do my business, I would first have to take myself abstractly, as a member of all society. And of course prove my orthodoxy.

The issue of property has been wrongly put. The question is not whether personality extends into the environment—of course it does—but what kind of personality a man has. If he is exclusive and squeamish and rides roughshod over people, then his property will also be like that and will be objectionable. If he imagines that huge holdings do not enclose the commons, exploit the common wealth, and deprive other people, he is a fool. If the Navy would explain to me how it is temporarily appropriating that stretch of water for an interesting experiment, I might feel that *my* property in that stretch of water is being improved. I would willingly cooperate. My horizon would no longer be obstructed.—To be sure, I distrust *any* experiments of the Navy, but that is another story.

Nor is the issue between "private property" and "social property." Who would want to be private? We exist mainly, though not altogether, in community relations. To be a private individual is largely pathological. For a society to act as a collective is largely pathological.

The error of those who are mistakenly called "conservative" is not their laissez-faire economics. It is probable that competitive free enterprise is a more productive system than mercantilism, monopoly capitalism, or socialist collectivism. But as in the past, free enterprises still parcel out the commons as if it were on the market. They treat moral, cultural, and esthetic affairs that belong to the community as if they were economic affairs, for example, giving access to the young, conserving the environment, helping the needy. But these are necessary for society to be tolerable at all. The tolerable background for any economic activity cannot be an object of economic activity.

And they make a corresponding mistake in their economics. In most of our present production, the chief value comes from the genius of Watt, Faraday, Rutherford, and so on; from the industry of our fathers who cleared the woods and laid out the roads; and from natural resources. We all happen to have inherited these gold mines. It is unreasonable for a few who control capital and thereby can make use of the inheritance, not to pay everybody royalties, for example, at least the guaranteed income.

Finally, in developed economies, both socialists and capitalists make a disastrous ethical mistake, mortgaging the present to the future. They put too much effort into profit, accumulating surpluses for new productivity and infrastructure, rather than first assuring a small profit for stability and livelihood. Growth Rate and Gross National Product become abstract fetishes, for which they sacrifice the present by skimping it, and take the life out of the future by overdetermining it.

Needless to say, the more the abstract Growth Rate flourishes, the more millions of people are likely to be left out and reduced to misery, for nobody pays attention to their petty concrete needs, which have nothing to do with Growth Rate and Gross National Product. There is a bigger pie to divide, but it can't be divided into inefficient items like food for a technologically displaced farmer or miner. In the long run he will surely be better off; in the fairly short run he will surely be quite dead.

Let me again quote the anecdote: "What," asked Coleridge, "about the little village that is rather self-sufficient and does not take part in the National Economy?" "Why, such a place is of no importance," said the Manchester economist. "Sir? are 500 Christian souls of no importance?"

In *Communitas* (Scheme III), we make the dumb-bunny suggestion of a dual economy with dual money: Let the big economy expand as madly as it wants, but see to it that there is also a small independent subsistence economy, producing subsistence goods at small-economy prices. (Recently, however, we have come to see that for ecological reasons the big economy can't expand like mad either.)

Equalitarians object to special privilege; for instance, they don't like it that my sheepskin promises to me "all the rights, privileges, and immunities" of a doctor of philosophy. But my ancestor Abelard and his students fought and suffered for those rights and immunities; we (maybe) need them to do our thing; I am not at all willing to renounce them—indeed, I am a stickler for them.

Again the issue is put wrongly. It would be better if every person and his community of interest had far more rights, privileges, and immunities. Children have special rights, privileges, and immunities. Those who have worn themselves out bringing up children have special rights, privileges, and immunities—I guiltlessly say, "Young man, tote my bag." As a writer I need liberties and immunities that do not belong to a man who will never write a line; he does not care about freedom of the press, and in fact he won't defend it. The real issue is that many rights, privileges, and immunities that once had an historical warrant and enhanced experience and activity, have now become a racket. For example, professionals do need a peer group and to be professionally responsible only to their peer group, their oath, and the nature of things; but the economic blackmail of the medical associations is a racket. Lily whites may have a claim to club and eat with the like-minded, but not to deprive blacks of a share in the common wealth by segregating a restaurant on the main street, a neighborhood of a thousand houses, a national industry.

Professionals are bound to develop a ritual and secret language and mystify the laity, but this is acceptable (within limits)—their thing *is* a mystery and they have to do it their own way. What is unacceptable is for them to get the State to certify them as the only legal practitioners and exempt themselves from competition and criticism. The pretext is to protect the public from quacks; the effect is to increase the number of quacks, including those who are certified.

I am suspicious of equal law for everybody, like the *jus gentium* of the Romans that emerged with an Empire from which no one could escape. It is safer to have a bewildering tangle of unique prerogatives, and lots of borders to cross.

The main reason that Jefferson was a champion of freehold farming as a way of life was that it was independent of political pressures. It kept open the possibility of anarchy that he hankered for—"Let Shays' men go. If you discourage mutiny, what check is there on government?" If a farmer doesn't like the trend, he can withdraw from the market, eat his own crops, and prudently stay out of debt. If he has a freehold, they can't throw him off his land. (In Jefferson's day, he couldn't be drafted.) Other kinds of tenure have a similar privilege, academic tenure or seniority on the job, but of course the whole enterprise can shut down.

My own admiration for farming is its competence. The wonderfully direct connection between causes and effects, whether the seeds, the soil, the weather, the breeding, the plumbing in the barn, or the engine of the tractor; and of course growing it and then eating it. Needless to say, a farmer understands most of this only empirically, practically, not scientifically. He is not altogether in control. That too is very good; there are gods.

And Wordsworth had a good insight of the beauty and morality of rural life. The ecology of a country scene is so exquisitely complicated that we finally have to take it as just given. This simplifies it morally, we can relax a little. But I can't take the traffic or housing in Manhattan as given; it is an artifact and I have to do something about it. Also, the country scene has been so worked over for millions of years that it is bound to have unity and style, heroic in scale, minute in detail. But for various well-known reasons, the man-made scene is bound to be ugly. If people change their ways, it could become at least modest.

Sciences are sacred because they devote themselves—indeed, in a priestly way—to the natures not made by us, so they enable us to make sense and not live wishes, hopes, and nightmares. Being observant, humble, and austerely self-denying, dedicated scientists accumulate the reward of their Calvinist virtues. Great powers flow through them—which they can use to our disadvantage. Therefore they ought to bind themselves by oath to benefit and not harm the community, and it is better if this oath is public and explicit, like the Hippocratic oath.

When, instead, they come on like petty clerks of the powers-that-be and as petty bankers of their own economic interests, the forces of nature are unleashed without human beings to interpret and exorcise them.

We others, artists and literary men, are easygoing toward nature and mix into our service a good deal of ourselves. So we accumulate little force, but it is domesticated. We do not need to bind ourselves with an oath, except not to censor.

Futurologists take current trends, that may or may not be good, and by extrapolating them for twenty years perform the sleight of hand of making them into norms that we must learn to conform to and prepare ourselves for. As a group they are extraordinarily slavish to the *status quo*—science fiction writers are often far more critical and daring. They seem to want to delete from primary experience its risky property of passing into the Next, beyond a horizon that very swiftly becomes dim and dark. Aristotle: "The past and present are necessary, the future is possible."

Luckily, human beings have enormous resources of anxiety, common sense, boredom, virtue, and perversity, to distort or reverse almost any trend you want.

The mania of planning for the future springs, of course, from the fact that current technology, urbanization, population, and communications are intractable—or at least the managers have lost their pragmatic inventiveness—so that it seems to be less desperate to grin and codify them. As Kafka advised, "Leopards break into the temple; make it part of the ritual."

My own prediction, however, is that there will be increasing disorder for twenty years, and that might be very well. Some things—some times—break up into fragments of just the right size and shape. People en masse learn only by being frightened anyway—ten thousand dead one morning of the smog, a city wiped out by an accidental bomb. It's not that we are stupid, but it takes a big fact, not a syllogism, to warrant a big response. If only the process of disorder is not aggravated by reactionary Law and Order, liberal Futurology, and radical Idealism.

I am bemused, as I spell out this politics of mine, at the consistent package of conservative biases, the ideology of a peasant or a small entrepreneur who carries his office and capital under his hat. Localism, ruralism, face-to-face organization, distrust of planning, clinging to property, natural rights, historical privileges and immunities, letters to the editor that view with alarm, carrying on the family craft, piecemeal reforms, make do, and let me alone.

No. It is not a possessive peasant nor a threatened small entrepreneur, but a small child who needs the security of routine. There is no father. Mother is away all day at work. He is self-reliant because he has to be. It is lonely, but nobody bugs him, and the sun is pouring through the window.

Where the emphasis in a philosophy of experience is on the foreground empirical facts, as in Dewey, we come out with a bias toward experiment and a politics of progressivism. Where the emphasis is on the phenomenology, the horizons and backgrounds of experience, we come out with conservation and conservatism. The difference is the old principle of acculturation from tribe to tribe: if the new item is a plough or a technique for baking pottery, it diffuses rapidly; if it is a change of tabu, child-rearing, or esthetics, it is resisted, it diffuses slowly or not at all.

Since as experience I want the concrete and finite, with structure and tendency, a Next so I can live on a little, and a dark surrounding, politically I want only that the children have bright eyes, the river be clean, food and sex be available, and nobody be pushed around. There must not be horrors that take me by the throat, so I can experience nothing; but it is indifferent to me what the Growth Rate is, or if some people are rich and others poor, so long as they are *pauvres*, decently poor, and not *misérables* (Péguy's distinction). I myself never found that much difference between being very poor and modestly rich.

Idolatry makes me uneasy. I don't like my country to be a Great Power. I am squeamish about masses of people enthusiastically building a New Society.

The great conservative solutions are those that diminish tension by changing 2 percent of this and 4 percent of that. When they work, you don't notice them. Liberals like to solve a problem by adding on a new agency and throwing money at it, a ringing statement that the problem has been solved. Radicals like to go to the root, which is a terrible way of gardening, though it is sometimes sadly necessary in dentistry.

> Schultz, the neighbor's big black dog,
> used to shit on our scraggly lawn,
> but we feed him marrow bones
> and he treats our lawn like his own home.

> The kids of Fulton Houses in New York
> smashed windows on our pretty block for spite;
> we gave them hockey sticks to play with
> and they smashed more windows.

> The dog is an anarchist like me,
> he has a careless dignity
> —that is, we never think about it,
> which comes to the same thing.

73

The kids are political like you,
they want to win their dignity. They won't.
But maybe their children will be friendly dogs
and wag their tails with my grandchildren.

3

Beyond My Horizon—
Words

I am willing, God, to say
just how it is with me,
    the prayer best I can.
    But look, again and again

to say that we are dying
—this message is boring.
    "No, you do not need
    to write that down," He said.

I have no further grief in me.
I can imagine, no, foresee
    the losses I will suffer yet,
    but my eyes do not get wet.

When once the brass is burnished, Sire,
there is no use of further fire,
    it is a mirror. But it can be melted,
    Sire, and destroyed.

It's a rudimentary experience I choose as mine, as if I were a simpler animal who doesn't have a long human memory, nameless yearning, creature anxiety, synoptic vision, and abstract language. How do I fill the gaps and make sense to myself? There are things that I do and say ritually, that go beyond experience. I can read them off as sentences, but they are empty of content. They are not perceptions, meanings, or feelings. They are theological, "the substance of things unseen."

I do not "believe" these theological sentences, that is much too intellectual a term. Not that I am skeptical by disposition; I am rather gullible. I entertain as likely almost any esoterica that people tell me with conviction, whether telepathy, orgone boxes, the Eucharist, or the revelations induced by psychedelic mushrooms. Having no wonders of my own, I marvel at other people's. Writing this, I have a sudden fellow feeling for Hume, who said he would walk a mile to hear Whitefield deliver one of his revival sermons. Except that we won't use these ideas as premises for anything that we might responsibly say or do.

I don't have a "faith," that is much too factual and erotic a term. I think of Karl Barth, one of the few modern writers whom I always read with empathy and pleasure, surfing on the wave of his thought, and his beautiful style speaks right to me. But he had a kind of substantial love affair with Jesus; and either Jesus made him happy or his faith did. My experience contains no such fact or feeling and I am tolerably unhappy.

Rather, I go along exactly with Kant in his little book on religion, "within the limits of mere reason." What I say here was already well said by him, that sticking to finite chunks of experience, it is inevitable to say words that go beyond their horizons and relate them to what surrounds them. But there is no sense to the spatial metaphors of "beyond" or "surround" any more than to other prepositional metaphors like "above" or "within," or to Kant's own nominative metaphors "things in themselves" and "symbols." Conversely, however, there is nothing in my finite experience that *prevents* me from saying such words! This gives me a crazy freedom of speech that I otherwise lack. Freer and crazier than if I were superstitious or had a faith. But of course nothing follows from this freedom empty and crazy.

The agnostic way of being of Hume and Kant is out of fashion these days, so people do not remember the positive exhilaration of it. (Today, nonbelievers are atheists.) Since the theological sentences of agnosticism are empty, it is possible to pick and choose and shape them, as the Deists, Unitarians, Universalists, and Ethical Culturists did, to be edifying. Or for poetry. Or just to live on a little.

Let me say again what I don't mean and do mean. "*Le coeur a ses raisons que la raison ne connaît point.*" This is crashingly true, but it is not what I mean. Pascal meant deep impulse, specifically his Christian impulse, as when Lawrence said,

"Follow your deepest impulse." It was high romance for a mathematician like Pascal to make Pascal's wager.

"*Credo quia absurdum*." This is a powerful defiant idea, underlining the quite certain folly and Pharisaism of human judgments and moral values, and preferring to throw oneself on the Wholly Other. Writing about Ishmael and other outcasts in my twenties, I used to affirm the antinomian version of absurdity: let us rebel and sin in order to be touched by something divine, if only God's wrath.

ANGEL: Hypocrite! do you not live and breathe by the daily gifts here and here given you?

ISHMAEL: So *You* say! when this mask of the world is stripped away, then shall we have full joy!

Nevertheless, though I am still not impressed by the wisdom or morality of righteous society, I am no longer tempted to deny what I think I do know, nor to act imprudently on principle.

But I like the safeguard of the Negative Theology of Jewish and Islamic philosophers—and from a different angle, of the Taoists. That whatever we say, is not true of God, nor is the contrary true. Simply, God is not a body and I know only about bodies, including myself. I mustn't take them as idols, including myself.

And yet—and yet—Why should I be fastidious of idols? What difference does it make? "Manlike my God I make." It makes no difference. But idolatry is stupid, and try as hard as I can, I cannot be stupider than I am.

Psychoanalytically, the obvious interpretation of inevitable but empty religious ideas is that they are obsessional rituals, like hand-washing or touching lampposts—their real meaning is repressed. I agree. Kant himself was the type of an anal character,

79

with his scrupulosity, his routine, his sometimes amazingly harsh and strict sense of duty, his classifying, his aversion to instinctual feelings.

Yet it was Kant. Through middle age and a good old age, his work flowed on spontaneous, vigorous, brave, endlessly inventive and continually maturing, minutely attentive and boldly synoptic, and with a fine rhythm of style. We have to ask if Kant's way of being obsessional is not a good way to cope with the nature of things, in order to live on a little. I repeat it: the proof of a sage is that he survives, he knows how. "To work out your allotted span and not perish in mid-career: this is knowing" (Chuang-tzu).

And there is something sweet in religious routines, once drained of the virulence of belief. The cozy religiosity of the Danes, benignly ineffectual, is a good background for guiltless sex and common-sense pacifism. Every human child is necessarily brought up among tribal myths old or new. We must of course use our wits as best we can and strictly affirm and act our best judgment; but it is harsh and imperious toward oneself to try to root out one's archaic symbols. Especially since in the field of myths, new is almost invariably worse.

Finally, there is a wide divergence between the agnostic Enlightenment and what has proved to be the history of positive Science. But from the beginning they had different aims. It was the idea of humanism and the Enlightenment—of Erasmus and Montaigne, Hume and Kant—that the purpose of philosophy is to get rid of superstition so that life can go on; philosophy has no content. But the idea of positive Science— consider the program and utopia of Francis Bacon—was to accumulate a system of self-correcting natural philosophy by which we can live happily, with a useful scientific technology.

80

Naturally, during the sixteenth and seventeenth centuries, when humanism and heroic science were undermining the orthodox dogma, they were close allies. Indeed, before and during the French Revolution, they were for a time disastrously identified; together, they seemed to *be* the Enlightenment. But the Rule of Reason enthroned at Notre Dame was bound to disappoint, if only because the scientists did not yet know enough.

Now two centuries later, however, when positive Science does know a wonderful and fearful amount, it has itself become the worldwide system of orthodox belief, heavily capitalized, recruited by a million trained minds — "there are more scientists alive today than since Adam and Eve." And it is hand in glove with the other powers-that-be.

It still disappoints, though its futurology promises infinite blessings. But to us threadbare men of letters, heirs of humanism and the Enlightenment, it is again the entrenched system served by a priestly caste, and it is again our duty to show how it is a superstition, so life can go on. (Oddly, the agnostic critique of Hume and Kant has become an intrinsic part of the orthodoxy, as conventional positivist logic.)

In his swan song, *The Conflict of the Faculties*, Kant spoke of philosophy as the "loyal opposition from the Left," whose duty was to harass the three positive Faculties of Law, Medicine, and Theology. I have no doubt that at present he would be criticizing the Faculties of Law, Medicine, and Scientific Technology.

For us who are thankful that we occupy only the ground that we cover with our two feet, the primary theological virtues are patience and fortitude, so said Kafka. (I think also of the comic portrait of Socrates firmly planted during the battle, not going out of his way to look for trouble, but every now and then giving

81

a hard knock.) No doubt those who have a different kind of experience require different virtues.

Patience is drawing on underlying forces; it is powerfully positive, though to a natural view it looks like just sitting it out. How would I persist against positive eroding forces if I were not drawing on invisible forces? And patience has a positive tonic effect on others; because of the presence of the patient person, they revive and go on, as if he were the gyroscope of the ship providing a stable ground. But the patient person himself does not enjoy it.

In a passage that I often repeat, Goethe speaks of that patient finite thing the Earth. "The poor Earth!—I evermore repeat it—a little sun, a little rain, and it grows green again." It has a tonic effect on us. So the Earth repeats it, Goethe repeats it, and I repeat it.

Kafka himself, to be sure, was not persistent in his finitude. He was invaded by terrible paranoiac abstractions. (I take him as what he wrote.) Then his serene obsessional defenses broke down and he could not finish his stories.

Fortitude is to persist in one's task with an extra ounce of strength, after one has exhausted one's resources. As we say it in American, fortitude is to stay in there pitching. As I recall how often I have done it in bleak ball games and I have seen others do it, I realize it is a mystery.

But it must be a man's own ball game, exhausting his own natural powers, otherwise I will not get the extra ounce of strength, more than I have.—I learned from the most grievous event of my life, Matty's death five years ago, that it is useful to persist in doing what is one's own thing, exhausting one's natural powers very quickly when, in such a case, one has little grip on his own life. I wrote repetitive little poems about the one subject. And I was upbraided by an uncharitable lady for making literature out of the death of my only son. (My eyes are suddenly full of tears, but I will write down this *too*.) So I venture to give advice to other people in mourning: be sure that what you are doing is yours and persist in doing it; in everything else, willingly break down, suddenly bawl, run away if you feel like it.

Plato's Socrates defines courage as having an idea, and I suppose this helps one transcend his natural fear. But my hunch is that Socrates — it is in one of the early dialogues — said something less abstract: if one is *in* the situation, identifying with its meaning, he does not have a structure for running away; it does not occur to him, he is occupied. Then he will have an extra ounce of strength. He doesn't know from where; he has no leisure to ask.

I notice that I keep recurring to my authors of the concrete, the finite, the intrinsic: Socrates, Goethe, Kant, Kafka when he was well. It shows me again that I cannot learn anything different, and it shows that what I say is mine to say.

But I could spell it out as "developing" and it would come to the same thing. In my teens I was a Platonist and I wrote a long paper on the place of myths in the Dialectic Method: the plot was that it is the purpose of dialectic to bring us to a pause, paralyzed by the *narke*, the man-o'-war, and then there is a myth to revive us. But the form of Platonism to which I temperamentally gravitated was Leibniz: the concrete monad and its molecular *petites perceptions*,

—the dainty noise of drop on drop
accumulates to be the ocean's roar.

This seemed to me compatible with Freud whom I was also reading, as my only pornography.

Soon Berkeley and Hume, however, seemed to me even more like home. They were matter-of-fact. And I went backward from Plato to Socrates and Heraclitus and Parmenides. Kant, "of course," solved all the problems. When I was subjected to a heavy dose of McKeon's reading of Aristotle, for my purposes it was the same philosophy. Evidently, in these notes, I still think so.

I later learned just enough from the positivists and phenomenologists to steer my middle course between them, in the wake of William James, who was real American.

Meantime, I was a hungry reader of the neo-Protestants— I remember Nygren, Otto, Schweitzer, and Barth; and Maimonides, and Lao-tzu. These have somehow permitted me to say the magic I need, like Kant or William James or Rank, but unlike Aristotle or Freud.

No. As I now think of all of them, and scores of other great authors, what stands out is the common enterprise: how to explain (or explain away) the matter-of-fact, the erotic, the abiding, and the unknown. How it is and what to do. It is possible that being a philosopher sets it up this way; or it is possible that it is this way for everybody and philosophers cope by spelling it out. I don't know.

Faith is having a world-for-me. That my experience is given. That it will continue to be given: the Next is not the brink of a precipice. Its structure has consequences that I can draw; there might be evidence to clarify the meaning if I attend. By faith I am not caged in my finite experience; it has an horizon rather than bars; so I speak of it as "roomy enough." I am not alone, only lonely.

It is a latitudinarian notion of faith, like being sane. Nearly everybody behaves as if he had a world. A child runs headlong as though there will be gravity and ground, though he does not have nearly enough experience to believe this as certain as he acts it; it is built into his constitution. A speaker has a hearer in his language community, he does not think about it. Noah planted a vineyard because the Lord promised with his rainbow that something would come of it, there wouldn't be another flood. A scientist pursues his method as though the evidence was not planted to deceive him. I go to an orgasm by faith, I will not fall apart or not come down. We fall asleep by faith. I suppose there is nothing we do that we do not do by faith. "We live by faith."

I am paraphrasing Anselm's or Descartes' ontological argument: however we do proves faith. But there are no grounds for the faith. I cannot find anything in my experience that I would call faith. It is like Kierkegaard's Postman: one cannot tell, looking at him, that he is a Christian.

Perhaps the animal feeling of faith is trust, and perhaps at first, faith and trust are the same, like a child's trust in grownups or a dog's trust. These look animal. There is feeling on the face of the Adam of Michelangelo, trust already clouded with melancholy. But it is the genius of our families and institutions to destroy trust. Only God can destroy faith.

The Reformers seem to be right in saying that faith produces works but there is nothing that we can do to give faith. We can certainly do a good deal to remedy institutions that destroy trust.

"To them who have shall be given; from those who have not shall be taken away even that which they have." Yes. The muscular lad plays rough and gets still stronger. A lovable person is loved and becomes still more open, radiant, and lovable. A person who is not anxious profits from psychoanalysis; an anxious person can afford to profit very little. And faith yields works. But the error of Geneva is to institutionalize this unfair distribution, coming on like God, deciding who is elect.

Theological hope is expecting the impossible. It is a terrible risk; as Goethe said, "By acting as though the impossible were possible, you soon make the possible impossible."

Certainly, for unlucky people like myself, natural hope — imagining, wishing, expecting — is an utter curse. It is disappointment. This has so often proved itself to me that I have almost come to understand how it works. I entertain a wild hope before I have laid a groundwork, or even *instead* of making a practical plan. My fantasy is an abstraction not in touch with the real situation, and it keeps me out of touch with it. In the order of my wishes, a random promise becomes a heated vision; in the order of other people's behavior, it has been quite forgotten. Most often when I am hopeful, nothing at all eventuates. If something does happen to eventuate, I am overwrought and act foolishly.

I do better, and suffer less, if I act with nonattachment, doing what is technically correct, expecting nothing; or acting generously, casting bread on the waters, expecting nothing. And if anything eventuates, if I cope with it like a present fact rather than the fulfillment of a wish.

Yet my extraordinary ineptitude contains a clue. A man could not possibly succeed so poorly unless he needed to fail. Either I am afraid to get what I wish for, so I see to it that I don't; that is, my excessive hope is a built-in prudence. Or I have despaired beforehand that my wish is what I want, and therefore I do not go about it practically to succeed. Yes, for the crazy glow of my hope, not its substance, is the color of what I really

86

want, which is not possibly in the offing. And the horrible sinking of my disappointment is not for what I wished for, but because I am again reminded that I am not in paradise.

Theological hope is not delusory but blind. It is for a new
heavens and new earth and I do not know the content of such
a change. As I live from day to day, I do not feel any such hope,
yet I live as if I had it.

> What do you want, my captain? what you want
> is impossible, therefore you must want nothing.
> "No. I am looking for the Northwest Passage to
> India; *if I had made the world,*
> *that would exist."*

Love is the experience that takes me beyond experience.
Love has a concrete object and feeling, but it exists by promis-
ing to continue beyond Here Now and Next. As Rilke's Unicorn
"exists by the possibility of being," love exists by the possibility
of becoming. Thus it is the only theological virtue that is not
empty of content, and from which something follows in my behavior. And I think this is why it has a privileged position in orthodox theology: it incarnates the god. He who will come.

To make a familiar distinction, sexual lust is experienced as
Here Now and Next, it does not include an indefinite hope. But
this difference, though real, is transient, for happy lust very soon
turns into sexual love or into love without sex. Conversely, I
doubt that one can have a good time lusting unless he is pre-
pared to risk loving, losing himself. Orgastic pleasure is already a
risk that needs both trust and faith. We love what has by-passed
our blocks, so unfamiliar energy is released, that feels like risk.

Theologians make too much of the distinction between *agape*, self-giving self-losing love, and *eros*, love that tries to satisfy oneself and complete oneself. For also the latter is self-losing. And common language has always refused to make the distinction. Simply, the beloved fills the field of experience — "I am That" — and because I am diminished, new energy wells up, undomesticated, indefinite in meaning. It is crazy hope, except that now it seems to be practical, possible, having something to work at.

All love, whether sexual, parental, communal, or compassionate, is delusional. There will be no such ever-new world, if only because my anxiety reasserts me and protects me. (Saints, of course, can keep going.) But whether it is delusional or not, love is psychotic. It can be quietly psychotic, as I reasonably and prudently give myself away piece by piece.

Love creates new faith. Faith is given by grace, and love does the work of grace. It does so by actively making, or making up, a world for me in which I trust and where hope has substance; paradise, where there is no difference between grace and everyday practical action.

I notice, as I write this, how well it is all told by the Christian myth of Jesus incarnate as love and redemptive by giving himself, instituting a new heavens and new earth. But by my character I natually prefer a literal analysis to the beautiful story.

I say "I love you" more than I do, not lying,
it's an hypothesis I hope will be surprisingly confirmed.

But there is no rime or reason for you to love me too.
Don't you say anything at all. Just be.

I like to announce my intentions with a fanfare of six trumpets.

I'm tickled when I sound like an old book.

The type of self-giving love is grown-ups' love of children. The unique gift that children give us is the opportunity to do for them, with no claim of return, therefore no resentment, therefore no guilt. It is depressing that this glaringly obvious fact is not told in the stories of God the Father, that *He* has a lot to be grateful for because of His creatures. Instead, He is represented as paternalistic; His guidance is very like a command, exacting obedience; His feeding seems to expect thanks.

On the other hand, those who, unlike the Creator of the animals, want to limit the number of children born, so that children may inherit an uncrowded Earth—they also tend to overlook that caring for children is one of the few things that make life important from day to day, and there ought to be enough opportunity to go around. Friendship and neighbor-love are pretty complicated to manage. The ideal love of the artist or scientist is a daily fact for only a few. Love of society or mankind is abstract and begins to stink of idolatry. But everybody can love children.

Compassion, the virtue of the physician, is another spectacularly self-losing love. It is psychotic denial; the physician denies that the patient is really as he is. (Psychoanalytically, the compassionate man refuses to accept his own maiming.) And like other lovers, the physician sometimes transforms the world by making his denial stick. He puts it into question, which is crazy after all, finite experience or love? But in my observation, physicians are deeply angry people: "How dare you walk into my office in that condition?"

—A lifeguard, when he rescues someone, curses.

He has nothing to show for having lost himself. It was just remedial.

When Isaac was saved on Mt. Moriah, Abraham must have gone into a towering anger. The Bible, written as God's history, tells us nothing about this. All that heartache for nothing.

Beauty too proves something beyond experience, but it is not practical. The forms of paradise without the matter. As Kant put it, if the forms are adapted to our experience, we cannot experience the adaptation but only the pleasure of it. The forms seem purposeful for us, but they have no purpose. Plato speaks of beautiful forms as memories, of the jewels in the court of Jove.

Beauty mild is lively, but strong is terrible. When a strong beauty is just to see or hear but not desire, it makes me cry because paradise is lost—and there is nothing to do. If it is something to desire, then it is at peril that I resist what attracts me, however dangerous, unavailable, inappropriate, or perverse I may judge it to be. I must love it and suffer rather than be bored and caged as the horizon closes in. I cannot choose my paradise to be convenient, moral, or prudent. Pursuing the beautiful, I become still more inept.

And then it is notorious that the beautiful appears only at the right esthetic distance and nearness. With art works, a good critic chooses the distance at which they show to best advantage. But with beautiful people, it is hard to attain the right distance, and impossible, I have found, to maintain it. One cannot eat beauty or fuck it. I have often lapsed into orgasm because the tension of beauty became intolerable for me. I have to sign it off.

The beautiful is not abstract; I cannot believe it is a delusion, and must respond with grief or desire; but it is only an esthetic surface, not practical for me.

It is like King Macbeth in the play: he is not an illusion of a king, he is a real king; but he is made of words, and one must not jump onto the stage and join in the battle. On the other hand, those contemporary plays in which I am supposed to join in, are not beautiful, and I get more excitement from action on the streets or with my friends. An artist can stage my beauty, but he cannot stage my paradise. A politician tries to stage my paradise, and it is the same purgatory.

I notice that I sometimes use the language of psychoanalysis and rarely a few terms of existential philosophy, but on the whole I prefer the language of orthodox theology to talk about the invisibles. Using words like faith, hope, love, paradise, purgatory, nonattachment, vocation, Way, Creation, koan, holy spirit, mana, Messiah, idol, Void, God, Karma, incarnation — mostly from the West, with a scattering from the East or from primitive religions.

These theological terms have been in use for thousands of years far and wide. We must assume that they have met a need, and they have certainly been polished by handling. Naturally they are resonant in a poet's vocabulary. They are very ambiguous and have been tormented by interpretation — though perhaps not more so than recent psychoanalytic and philosophical terms — but the contrasting interpretations are themselves ancient and have been spelled out in schisms and heresies. Hundreds of fine brains have been busy about it, with millions of adherents, and much bloodshed to show that they meant something or other.

If I use this language when I talk to a person brought up in a Christian sect, we often quickly come to an earnest conversation about important matters of life or death. Using the other languages with no matter whom proves to be pedantic, cruder, and more polemical. To be sure, some Christians are puzzled and disappointed that, since we understand one another, I do not come out where they do. Richard McKeon, the Aristotelian, used to have this trouble with the neo-Thomists at the University of Chicago during the thirties; they charitably called him the Anti-Christ, because by making better sense of the texts he sometimes cooled off prospective converts.

Needless to say, the ones who are irritated if I say "holy spirit" or "Messiah" are the Unitarians and Ethical Culturists. Having (once) struggled to get rid of superstitious beliefs, they cannot tolerate even the language of theology.

But young people these days like this palaver, which seems meaningful to them, though their language is rather more eclectic than mine. There is a difference from my own youth when such talk was considered moronic and we had no language at all to describe our hopes or troubles. (I hit on psychoanalysis.) In the peculiar historical crisis they are now in, some of the young are so alienated that they finally germinate crazy ideas and will add to the history of theology, if there is any further history of anything.

Paradise is the world practicable. I do not mean happy, nor even practical so that I can make it work, but simply that I can work *at* it, without being frustrated beforehand. A task to wake up toward. If I work at something, I am happy enough while I am doing it—I don't think about whether or not I am happy. And if I have worked at it, if I have tried, I sleep well even if I have failed.

This is a very modest criterion of paradise. To many people (how would I know?), there might be no reason to call such a world miraculous rather than the nature of things. For instance, John Dewey, who must have been a happy man, describes the nature of things as pragmatic through and through. But though I have faith that there is a world for me, I am foreign in it, I cannot communicate my needs, I do not share the customs, I am inept. So it is like a new world, I am as if resurrected, when the world is practicable. Therefore, until that moment, I put a premium on patience and fortitude.

The difficulties of the world, said Kafka, are mathematical. Given the spreading of space in all directions on a plane, it is infinitely more probable that our paths will diverge than converge. That you will be out when I phone and I will be out when you ring my bell — indeed, as Kafka points out, I was on my way over to your place. If several conditions are necessary for success, and each is moderately probable, the likelihood of their combination is wildly improbable. At every relay the message is distorted, and we did not speak the same dialect to begin with, but just enough of the same language so that we thought we were communicating. An unexpected stress, a lapse of attention, makes me vulnerable to other stresses, breakdowns, and accidents, so the rate of mishap is exponential. You get a flat tire and pull over, and step out over the edge and break a leg. These are the facts of life, no?

They are the facts of life for those who cannot abstract, who have only concrete and finite experience, like Kafka and me. We cannot take the vast numbers of possibilities as collective facts to manage, assigning them the infinite numbers Aleph, Beth, and Gimel. We cannot soar off the ground covered by our own two feet in order to survey the landscape. Since we have

no values except in the tendency of what we are doing, we cannot make a plan of action to a far goal; we have no such goal,
just the reality that we are dissatisfied. Then except by the miracle that events happen to converge in my poor Here Now and
Next, my world is impracticable.

Fortunately, I have low standards of what is excellent as
happiness.

In my politics—anarchist, decentralist, planning to leave
out as much as possible, strongly conservative of simple goods
that in fact exist—I have hit on a principle: Given the mathematical improbability of happiness, for God's sake don't add
new obstacles.

In my morals, the cardinal sin is waste.

Consider the logistics of sexual satisfaction, a major part of
happiness for most of us. Starting with the odd notion of sexual
intercourse as a way of reproducing species, there is a rough carpenter's logic in dividing the human males and females equally,
50-50, to maximize the couplings; and then to attach a strong instinctual drive so that the animals will seek one another and persist in accomplishing the complicated operation of approaching,
getting an erection, finding the hole, being receptive, and so
forth. But a desire that is attached can become detached. The
50-50 possibilities are immediately drastically reduced by notions
of beauty, inevitable childhood nostalgias and tabus, insecurities
caused by factors that have nothing to do with sexuality, fetishism
of other poles and holes. Since it is a complicated mechanism,
Murphy's Law will certainly hold: if the parts can be put together
wrong, they will be. And the machine has to operate in the frame
of the rest of life and social life: being hungry and sleepy, sick,
maimed, hampered by institutions and laws, poor and disadvan-

taged. Of course, since nature always operates with prodigal generosity and calculated waste, with a factor of safety in the thousands and millions, in spite of everything the human species is reproduced. The chances of personal happiness are trivial.

I have had half-a-dozen too brief love affairs (I am past 60), and in every case our virtue was to be practical, seizing chance opportunities, creating no obstacles, having no ideas in our minds, and trying hard to make one another happy. Or put it this way: I offer myself all at once as a package, with the absurd conditions of my ineptitude, my fantasies, my perverse needs, and my crazy hope. I must be either frightening or ludicrous. But the one who became my lover was not put off and took me at face value. *Then* we were practical. And I say proudly, when we could not continue indefinitely as is the essence of love, the causes of our separation were not our doing, they were mathematical.

This world is purgatory. I have plenty of proof that I am not damned — I understand that it is heretical to say so — but I am being tried, I have no notion why. Maybe that's what I'm supposed to learn. Faith, having this-world-for-me, means that I am not tried beyond my capacity. The Lord will keep me alive, until He won't.

I spoke of myself as "unlucky," but it's not exact. Rather, my destiny has been to be continually hungry, balked, and deprived, but never starved, a total failure, with nothing. Continually in pain and handicapped by it, rarely incapacitated. Since I cannot believe that God is playing games with me, He must be testing me for my own good. Perhaps He is protecting me from the excesses of happiness, but gives me enough to keep me alive. If this is the case, He doesn't understand me well. For I do not become foolish, lazy, or arrogant, but sensible and grateful when I am

happy, whereas this purgatorial regime keeps me inept and grip-
ing. Maybe I am wrong and if I were very happy I would be arrogant. I can't conceive what that would be like.

Sometimes I have the thought that God means to provide
for me better but He can't. There are shortages. He doesn't
have the technique to deal with difficult cases like me. He does
well, considering.

Or I have the bitter, but not hostile, thought that God is an
impatient artist. His conceptions are sublime beyond anything,
like War Horse or the Big Dipper. Or they are deliciously odd, like
wrapping up a bundle of levers, tubes, and wires—mechanics,
hydrostatics, and electronics—to be an animal. The execution is
usually exquisitely minute. Yet there are clumsy or unfinished
sentences, missing transitions, characters left hanging.

However it is, since I am in purgatory, I sing "Lead Kindly
Light—one step enough for me." I often hum variations on the
tune of it, half a dozen, a dozen, twenty, as I walk along.

There is a Creation, given to me. In which "everything is
what it is and not another thing" (Bishop Butler).

I have tried to experience this givenness by dumb-bunny
experiments. For instance, I am in the waiting-room, roughly
aware of the rough structure of my chunk of experience. Can I
notice the new that occurs that is not in that structure, and that
will be given? A side door opens and a Puerto Rican woman in
a green dress emerges. The effect is paranoiac; her appearance
is portentous, a "delusion of reference," more tightly structured
than all the rest. I dare not let the new be new.

The givenness of experience is what I do *not* attend to as I
walk along, and there is always new space for it coming into
being. Or when I pay attention to a meaning, and there is

surprisingly more meaning, or less meaning, than I thought. Or I open my eyes, and I must take up from where I have been thrown. To Adam, I conjecture, the givenness of Creation was more apparent; everything happened to him for the first time. He lived in surprise. The givenness of Creation is surprise. But one cannot be surprised in the way one chooses to be surprised.

Kant, like Aristotle, held that existence is not a proper predicate that makes a scientific difference. There is no property of a real thing that may not be assigned to an imaginary thing and yet not make it real. Givenness is essential to any experience, but it cannot be experienced as such, nor scientifically measured. I must respect this opinion. Yet is is hard not to speculate that there is some extra energy in what is real rather than a possibility, a wish, or a dream. There are such heavy consequences from the reality of the real. Why could not this extra fire be measured, like the heat that changes water into steam? Possibility is one "phase"; add the elixir and wish is another "phase"; and existing is another "phase."

I cannot think something into becoming real. But a reality can certainly make me think.

The present, says Whitehead, is holy ground. It is strange. It not only has the crashing weight of reality, but, unlike the immobile real past, it is frothing into indefinite possibilities. It is the Burning Bush of Moses that was not consumed, out of which God named Himself "Who Am."

It is the aim of Zen Buddhist exercises to know presentness as an experience, and it is said to be a mighty revelation. But of course the koan that brings infinite enlightenment is just the specious present: "What is the Buddha?" "Pass the salt." I have not been enlightened. (How would I know?)

In our Western tradition, however, both of the Jews and the Greeks, we have methodically won a mighty revelation of the Creation which we sum up by saying, There is a nature of things. *"Felix qui potuit rerum cognoscere causas."* By methodically studying the present appearances, we come to know, not the present, but the reality.

The Easterner seems to say that the present is God, the Westerner that it is the sacred text.

In *The Galley to Mytilene* I tried to distinguish the Actuality that weighs down the ship carrying the message of doom; the Reality of the confusion of the sailors in which the ship is foundering; and the Existing Moment on whose wings the new ship is bringing the message of clemency. But it is the same ship. I wrote, "Try! and I shall never be able to distinguish them."

History, what has happened and happens, has a privileged position over possibilities, noble ideas, lost causes. It is Creation, and thenceforth the given. And I can understand why Vico, Hegel, and the others have taken it to be God or His demiurge. But I think that these philosophers too much mean by history the history of institutions, nations, great men, Society. If God is history, it includes the history of me.

The Creator Spirit visits me and treats me as a familiar, but I have not experienced this. I have never felt inspired. (I think of Cupid and Psyche.)

After a work is finished, I can usually show in fine detail how it is made, how the parts hang together, and why it works; and I can often offer shrewd guesses as to why I made it, what it has done for me, and what it is for. But none of this is experienced by me while the work is in progress. And indeed, the words and their relations, and the choices to be made, are so indefinitely numerous that it is mathematically impossible that I could manage them, except to keep at it and to steer.

The coming of spirit is new creation. From nothing. In fields where I have any firsthand acquaintance, literature, social institutions, therapy, the relation of master and apprentice, the conservation of energy is not *prima facie*; it is far-fetched. Nobody in such fields would think of it. The weight of evidence is overwhelming that there are continual flashes of creation, order made from nothing, against entropy. There are initiative, invention, and insight, and there are routine, falling apart, and entropy, but the entropy does not look like the dominant trend. We would not see the passage of the prophetic into the bureaucratic if we were not struck by the prophetic. Sudden and interesting. My bias is to deny the theory of conservation.

The question is if the physicists who affirm conservation are not using it as an *a priori* principle, proving it beforehand by their language of equations and by their attitude toward the matter they work on, which is always *natura naturata*, never *natura naturans*. If they included themselves presently experimenting in their operational account of the experimental situation—as indeed the operational language requires—maybe they would come out differently. I don't know.

I think that a physics without the conservation of energy would look like Taoist magic. It might even be technologically productive. They say that the Master rode the whirlwind, the only one motionless in the storm.

I do not know of any sacraments that take me beyond experience. Love takes us beyond experience, but we love by grace, and I am puzzled at those who urge me to love my neighbor (though I think I ethically understand what it means to be a sociable, considerate, and cooperative neighbor).

Yet there are two religious exercises that confront the invisibles: confusion and prayer. It is odd to call confusion an exercise.

Experience is torn by confusion, and the darkness seeps through. "All have smiles on their faces, as if going up to the Spring Festival," says Lao-tzu, "only I am murky and confused." Murky, with the solemn face of an animal, not much in its mind. But confused because, unlike the animal, the sage has little grip on life, so his experience doesn't make sense, it has no tendency. He is standing out of the way.

The sage is at a loss on ordinary occasions; he does not need "borderline situations" in order to go blank.

Buddhists and Western contemplatives attain clarity by their nonattachment. Therefore I say they are abstract; by concentration they have willed themselves out of the stream. The Taoist sage is scattered—drowning—as he relaxes his grip on life. His insight becomes still dimmer than it was, and he is face to face with the void. Which may or may not yield up a treasure.

For those of us who are used to making sense, however, it takes a big deal to be baffled. Typically, we have tragic dilemmas, the clashing of absolute duties. To carry these through is very much a Western plot. In the *Gita*, when Arjuna is in a tragic dilemma, the Lord advises him to act with nonattachment, and evil will not cling to him any more than water to the lotus leaf. But the recipe of our Greek tragic plots is decently to affirm both contradictions, to sink into them deeper, till the protagonist becomes exhausted and then confused and then goes blank, all with a good conscience. As Kant says, it is one of the functions of God—not my business—to see to it that, if

I do my duty, I can nevertheless be happy. "You do not need to finish the task," said Rabbi Tarfon more gently, "neither are you free to leave it off."

When we are baffled on a grand political, national scale, we hope for the coming of Messiah. For instance, the probability is high (95 percent) that atom bombs will destroy my friends and children. Our statesmen are not going to solve this (100 percent). Yet we persist in our institutions because of the coming of Messiah.

Statistically, as I grow old, I inevitably see more and more the death of my colleagues and dear ones, and I am confused. I understand that all flesh is as the grass, and very good. I see, too, the ever unique woe the survivors suffer—what we knew as moving and responding and initiating movement, is a worthless corpse, and it is too late for many things; yet I understand, I *understand* that we must try to mourn it through. I understand these two ideas but I cannot grasp them in one vision. It is too sublime for my finite experience and I become confused.

Prayer is the opposite exercise. I gather together my finite experience that is scattering in confusion. Here it all is, like an offering. Thus I disown my experience and again come face to face with nothing.

I do not pray for anything; whom would I ask? When I am not needy but happy, there is also no one to thank. But I pray by saying just how it is with me, and that is my prayer.

If we pay close attention to an isolated word, instead of scanning it in use in an ongoing sentence, it becomes odd and crazy. It is the same with any object that we gaze at intently, unless it is something beautiful and loved that keeps meeting us with new meanings. (But even such a thing soon becomes exhausted and looks monstrous.) So, by publishing my chunk of experience as literally as I can, I get rid of it.

Unfortunately, I have then thrown it to you, like the Orthodox confession in the village square.

When I do what is called "thinking," muttering to myself, I never use words like God or Faith, and they are in no way premises for my behavior. When I talk to other people, I sometimes use them, but not authentically; I might use such language, as I have said, to facilitate earnest conversation with a believer, though I am not a believer; or I might use it to cut short a boring conversation with an unbeliever, when I am too tired to explain myself better. When I write, however, I readily use this vocabulary and apparently seriously. How is this?

In "*Apology for Literature*," I suggest a possible reason: "Maybe it is that when I think or talk to myself, I am embarrassed; but when I write, I am not embarrassed"—since writing is my free act. But there could be a simpler reason, more *prima facie*, more what it feels like; I use this language because it is a poetic convention, a traditional jargon, like wearing old clothes because they are comfortable. It means nothing. A free act is an empty act, except as an act. It means what is the genius of the language of billions of human speakers—not my business. As a writer my business is only to be as clear as possible and say a work that has a beginning, middle, and end.

4

Being Queer

Jail and blows, being a coward,
I dread, but I am inured
    to be misunderstood
    because the common reason, God,

communes with me. Let them refute
the propositions I have put
    with nail and hammer on the door
    where people pass, upon the square.

In ESSENTIAL WAYS, my homosexual needs have made me a nigger. Most obviously, of course, I have been subject to arbitrary brutality from citizens and the police; but except for being occasionally knocked down, I have gotten off lightly in this respect, since I have a good flair for incipient trouble and I used to be nimble on my feet. What makes me a nigger is that it is not taken for granted that my out-going impulse is my right. Then I have the feeling that it is not my street.

I don't complain that my passes are not accepted; nobody has a claim to be loved (except small children). But I am degraded for making the passes at all, for being myself. Nobody likes to be rejected, but there is a way of rejecting someone that accords him his right to exist and is the next best thing to accepting him. I have rarely enjoyed this treatment.

Allen Ginsberg and I once pointed out to Stokely Carmichael how we were niggers, but he blandly put us down by saying that we could always conceal our disposition and pass. That is, he accorded us the same lack of imagination that one accords to niggers; we did not really exist for him. Interestingly, this dialogue was taking place on (British) national TV, that haven of secrecy. More recently, since the formation of the Gay Liberation Front, Huey Newton of the Black Panthers has welcomed homosexuals to the revolution, as equally oppressed.

In general in America, being a queer nigger is economically and professionally not such a disadvantage as being a black nigger, except for a few areas like government service, where there is considerable fear and furtiveness. (In more puritanic regimes, like present day Cuba, being queer is professionally and civilly a bad deal. Totalitarian regimes, whether communist or fascist, seem to be inherently puritanic.) But my own experience has been very mixed. I have been fired three times because of my queer behavior or my claim to the right to it, and these are the only times I have been fired. I was fired from the University of Chicago during the early years of Robert Hutchins; from Manumit School, an offshoot of A. J. Muste's Brookwood Labor College; and from Black Mountain College. These were highly liberal and progressive institutions, and two of them prided themselves on being communities. — Frankly, my experience of radical community is that it does not tolerate my freedom. Nevertheless, I am all for community because it is a human thing, only I seem doomed to be left out.

On the other hand, so far as I know, my homosexual acts and the overt claim to them have never disadvantaged me much in more square institutions. I have taught at half a dozen State universities. I am continually invited, often as chief speaker, to conferences of junior high school superintendents, boards of Regents, guidance counsellors, task forces on delinquency, and so forth. I say what I think is true — often there are sexual topics; I make passes if there is occasion: and I seem to get invited back. I have even sometimes made out — which is

106

more than I can say for conferences of SDS or the Resistance. Maybe the company is so square that it does not believe, or dare to notice, my behavior; or more likely, such professional square people are more worldly (this is our elderly word for "cool") and couldn't care less what you do, so long as they don't have to face anxious parents and yellow press.

As one grows older, homosexual wishes keep one alert to adolescents and young people more than heterosexual wishes do, especially since our society strongly discountenances affairs between older men and girls or older women and boys. And as a male, the homosexual part of one's character is a survival of early adolescence anyway. But needless to say, there is a limit to this bridging of the generation gap. Inexorably I, like other men who hang around campuses, have found that the succeeding waves of freshmen seem more callow and incommunicable and one stops trying to rob the cradle. Their music leaves me cold. After a while my best contact with the young has gotten to be with the friends of my own grown children, as an advisor in their politics, rather than by my sexual desires. (The death of my son estranged me from the young world altogether.)

On the whole, although I was desperately poor up to a dozen years ago—I brought up a family on the income of a share-cropper—I don't attribute this to being queer but to my perva-sive ineptitude, truculence, and bad luck. In 1945, even the Army rejected me as "Not Military Material" (they had such a stamp) not because I was queer but because I made a nuisance of myself with pacifist action at the examination and also had bad eyes and piles.

Curiously, however, I have been told by Harold Rosenberg and the late Willie Poster that my sexual behavior used to do me damage in precisely the New York literary world. It kept me from being invited to advantageous parties and making contacts to get published. I must believe Harold and Willie because they were unprejudiced observers. What I myself noticed in the thirties and forties was that I was excluded from the profitable literary circles dominated by Marxists in the thirties and ex-Marxists in the forties because I was an anarchist. For example, I was never invited to PEN or the Committee for Cultural Freedom. When CCF finally got around to me at the end of the fifties, I had to turn them down because they were patently tools of the CIA. (I said this in print in '61, but they lied their way out.)

To stay morally alive, a nigger uses various kinds of spite, which is the vitality of the powerless. He may be randomly destructive, since he feels he has no world to lose, and maybe he can prevent the others from enjoying their world. Or he may become an in-group fanatic, feeling that only his own kind are authentic and have soul. There are queers and blacks belonging to both these parties. Queers are "artistic," blacks have "soul." (This is the kind of theory, I am afraid, that is self-disproving; the more you believe it, the stupider you become; it is like trying to prove that you have a sense of humor.) In my own case, however, being a nigger seems to inspire me to want a more elementary humanity, wilder, less structured, more variegated, and where people pay attention to one another. That is, my plight has given energy to my anarchism, utopianism, and Gandhianism. There are blacks in this party too.

My actual political stance is a willed reaction-formation to being a nigger. I act that "the society I live in is mine," the title of one of my books. I regard the President as my public servant whom I pay, and I berate him as a lousy employee. I am more

Constitutional than the Supreme Court. And in the face of the gross illegitimacy of the Government—with its Vietnam War, military-industrial cabal, and C.I.A.—I come on as an old-fashioned patriot, neither supine nor more revolutionary than is necessary for my modest goals. This is a quixotic position. Sometimes I sound like Cicero.

In their in-group, Gay Society, homosexuals can get to be fantastically snobbish and a-political or reactionary. This is an understandable ego-defense: "You gotta be better than somebody," but its payoff is very limited. When I give talks to the Mattachine Society, my invariable sermon is to ally with all other libertarian groups and liberation movements, since freedom is indivisible. What we need is not defiant pride and self-consciousness, but social space to live and breathe. The Gay Liberation people have finally gotten the message of indivisible freedom, but they have the usual fanaticism of the Movement.

But there is a positive side. In my observation and experience, queer life has some remarkable political values. It can be profoundly democratizing, throwing together every class and group more then heterosexuality does. Its promiscuity can be a beautiful thing (but be prudent about VD).

I have cruised rich, poor, middle class, and petit bourgeois; black, white, yellow, and brown; scholars, jocks, Gentlemanly C's, and dropouts; farmers, seamen, railroad men, heavy industry, light manufacturing, communications, business, and finance; civilians, soldiers and sailors, and once or twice cops. (But probably for Oedipal reasons, I tend to be sexually anti-Semitic, which is a drag.) There is a kind of political meaning, I guess, in the fact that there are so many types of attractive human beings; but what is more significant is that the many functions in which I am professionally and economically engaged are not altogether cut and dried but retain a certain animation and sensuality. HEW in Washington and IS 201 in Harlem are not total wastes, though I talk to the wall in both. I have something to occupy me on trains and buses and during the increasingly long waits at airports. At vacation resorts, where people are idiotic because they are on vacation, I have a reason to frequent the waiters, the boatmen, the room clerks, who are working for a living. I have something to do at peace demonstrations—I am not inspirited by guitar music—though no doubt the TV files and the FBI with their little cameras have pictures of me groping somebody. The human characteristics that are finally important to me and can win my lasting friendship are quite simple: health, honesty, not being cruel or resentful, being willing to come across, having either sweetness or character on the face. As I reflect on it now, only gross stupidity, obsessional cleanliness, racial prejudice, insanity, and being habitually drunk or high really put me off.

In most human societies, of course, sexuality has been one more area in which people can be unjust, the rich buying the poor, males abusing females, sahibs using niggers, the adults exploiting the young. But I think this is neurotic and does not give the best satisfaction. It is normal to befriend and respect what gives you pleasure. St. Thomas, who was a grand moral philosopher though a poor metaphysician, says that the chief human use of sex—as distinguished from the natural law of procreation—is to get to know other persons intimately. That has been my experience.

A common criticism of homosexual promiscuity, of course, is that, rather than democracy, it involves an appalling superficiality of human conduct, so that it is a kind of archetype of

110

the inanity of mass urban life. I doubt that this is generally the case, though I don't know; just as, of the crowds who go to art-galleries, I don't know who are being spoken to by the art and who are being bewildered further—but at least some are looking for something. A young man or woman worries, "Is he interested in me or just in my skin? If I have sex with him, he will regard me as nothing": I think this distinction is meaningless and disastrous; in fact I have always followed up in exactly the opposite way and many of my lifelong personal loyalties had sexual beginnings. But is this the rule or the exception? Given the usual coldness and fragmentation of community life at present, my hunch is that homosexual promiscuity enriches more lives than it desensitizes. Needless to say, if we had better community, we'd have better sexuality too.

I cannot say that my own promiscuity (or attempts at it) has kept me from being possessively jealous of some of my lovers—more of the women than the men, but both. My experience has not borne out what Freud and Ferenczi seem to promise, that homosexuality diminishes this voracious passion, whose cause I do not understand. But the ridiculous inconsistency and injustice of my attitude have sometimes helped me to laugh at myself and kept me from going overboard.

Sometimes it is sexual hunting that brings me to a place where I meet somebody—for example, I used to haunt bars on the waterfront; sometimes I am in a place for another reason and incidentally hunt—for example, I go to the TV studio and make a pass at the cameraman; sometimes these are both of a piece—for example, I like to play handball and I am sexually interested in fellows who play handball. But these all come to the same thing, for in all situations I think, speak, and act pretty much the same. Apart from ordinary courteous adjustments of vocabulary—but not of syntax, which alters character—I say the same say and do not wear different masks or find myself suddenly with a different personality. Perhaps there are two opposite reasons why I can maintain my integrity: on the one hand, I have a strong enough intellect to see how people are for real in our only world, and to be able to get in touch with them despite differences in background; on the other hand, I am likely so shut in my own preconceptions that I don't even notice glaring real obstacles that prevent communication.

How I do come on hasn't made for much success. Since I don't use my wits to manipulate the situation, I rarely get what I want out of it. Since I don't betray my own values, I am not ingratiating. My aristocratic egalitarianism puts people off unless they are secure enough in themselves to be also aristocratically egalitarian. Yet the fact I am not phony or manipulative has also kept people from disliking or resenting me, and I usually have a good conscience. If I happen to get on with someone, there is not a lot of lies and bullshit to clear away.

Becoming a celebrity in the past few years, however, seems to have hurt me sexually rather than helped me. For instance, decent young collegians who might like me and who used to seek me out, now keep a respectful distance from the distinguished man. Perhaps they are now sure that I *must* be interested in their skin, not in them. And the others who seek me out just because I am well known seem to panic when it becomes clear that I don't care about that at all, and I come on as myself. Of course, a simpler explanation of my worsening luck is that I'm growing older every day, probably uglier, and certainly too tired to try hard.

As a rule I don't believe in poverty and suffering as a way of learning anything, but in my case the hardship and starvation

112

of my inept queer life have usefully simplified my notions of what a good society is. As with any other addict who cannot get an easy fix, they have kept me in close touch with material hunger. So I cannot take the Gross National Product very seriously, nor status and credentials, nor grandiose technological solutions, nor ideological politics, including ideological liberation movements. For a starving person, the world has got to come across in kind. It doesn't. I have learned to have very modest goals for society and myself: things like clean air, green grass, children with bright eyes, not being pushed around, useful work that suits one's abilities, plain tasty food, and occasional satisfying nookie.

A happy property of sexual acts, and perhaps especially of homosexual acts, is that they are dirty, like life: as Augustine said, *Inter urinas et feces nascimur*, we're born among the piss and shit. In a society as middle class, orderly, and technological as ours, it's good to break down squeamishness, which is an important factor in what is called racism, as well as in cruelty to children and the sterile exiling of the sick and aged. And the illegal and catch-as-catch-can nature of much homosexual life at present breaks down other conventional attitudes. Although I wish I could have had my parties with less apprehension and more unhurriedly, yet it has been an advantage to learn that the ends of docks, the backs of trucks, back alleys, behind the stairs, abandoned bunkers on the beach, and the washrooms of trains are all adequate samples of all the space there is. For both bad and good, homosexual life retains some of the alarm and excitement of childish sexuality.

It is damaging for societies to check any spontaneous vitality. Sometimes it is necessary, but rarely; and certainly not

113

homosexual acts which, so far as I have heard, have never done any harm to anybody. A part of the hostility, paranoia, and automatic competitiveness of our society comes from the inhibition of body contact. But in a very specific way, the ban on homosexuality damages and depersonalizes the educational system. The teacher-student relation is almost always erotic.— The only other healthy psychological motivations are the mother-hen relevant for small children and the professional who needs apprentices, relevant for graduate schools.— If there is fear and to-do that erotic feeling might turn into overt sex, the teacher-student relation lapses or, worse, becomes cold and cruel. And our culture sorely lacks the pedagogic sexual friendships, homosexual, heterosexual, and lesbian, that have starred other cultures. To be sure, a functional sexuality is probably incompatible with our mass school systems. This is one among many reasons why they should be dismantled.

I recall when *Growing Up Absurd* had had a number of glowing reviews, finally one irritated critic, Alfred Kazin, darkly hinted that I wrote about my Puerto Rican delinquents (and called them "lads") because I was queer for them. News. How could I write a perceptive book if I didn't pay attention, and why should I pay attention to something unless, for some reason, it interested me? The motivation of most sociology, whatever it is, tends to produce worse books. I doubt that anybody would say that my observations of delinquent adolescents or of collegians in the Movement have been betrayed by infatuation. But I do care for them.— Of course, *they* might say, "With such a friend, who needs enemies?"

Yet it is true that an evil of the hardship and danger of queer life in our society, as with any situation of scarcity and starvation, is that we become obsessional and one-track-minded about it. I have certainly spent far too many anxious hours of my life fruitlessly cruising, which I might have spent sauntering for other purposes or for nothing at all, pasturing my soul. But I trust that I have had the stamina, or stubbornness, not to let my obsession cloud my honesty. So far as I know, I have never praised a young fellow's bad poem because he was attractive. But of course I am then especially pleased if it is good and I can say so. And best of all, of course, if he is my lover and he shows me something that I can be proud of and push with an editor. Yes, since I began these reflections on a bitter note, let me end them with a happy poem that I like, from *Hawkweed*:

> We have a crazy love affair
> it is wanting each other to be happy.
> Since nobody else cares for that
> we try to see to it ourselves.
>
> Since everybody knows that sex
> is part of love, we make love.
> When that's over, we return
> to shrewdly plotting the other's advantage.
>
> Today you gazed at me, that spell
> is why I choose to live on.
> God bless you who remind me simply
> of the earth and sky and Adam.
>
> I think of such things more than most
> but you remind me simply. Man,
> you make me proud to be a workman
> of the Six Days, practical.

On balance, I don't know whether my choice, or compulsion, of a bisexual life has made me especially unhappy or only averagely unhappy. It is obvious that every way of life has its hang-ups, having a father or no father, being married or single, being strongly sexed or rather sexless, and so forth; but it is hard to judge what other people's experience has been, to make a comparison. I have persistently felt that the world was not made for me, but I have had good moments. And I have done a lot of work, have brought up some beautiful children, and have gotten to be 58 years old.

5

Apology
for Literature

Page after page I have lived Your world
in the narrative manner, Lord,
    in my own voice I tell Your story.
    Needless to say, I envy

people who dramatically
act the scenes of Your play.
    Even so, the narrative manner
    is my *misère et grandeur*.

It is our use
that some of us
    insist on how
    it is from our point of view.

STATEMENTS IN LITERARY WORKS are taken seriously and men of letters are invited to confer with experts as if they had something useful to contribute. They are not scientific statements. They are grounded in something, but in what? It is not exactly evidence. What kind of statement *is* it that men of letters make? What is their warrant for making it? I think the warrant is in the literary process itself.

There are innumerable books on works of literature and the lives of their authors, and there are many books on the philosophy of art. But to my surprise, I cannot think of a comprehensive study of the literary process—what it is to write books—drawn from what men of letters do. Like language itself, literature easily attaches to any subject-matter, yet it is less free-floating than language; criticism deals with whole concrete works. (In this respect, literature is not like grammar, rhetoric, and logic, which are "universal arts," as Aristotle called them, that are used for every purpose.) And literature has its own specific discipline, of writing the essay *through*, with a beginning, a middle, and an end.

Let me spell out these characteristics of literature and compare them with other disciplines, and see if they add up to a warrant for stating anything meaningful and true.

Like everybody else, a writer has a day-to-day life; but unlike any scientist or almost any professional, a writer's daily life and course of life are relevant to his special work and may at any time appear in his sentences. He may say, "My experience has been that..." or "For instance, yesterday I had a quarrel with my daughter and..." I can think of only pastoral theology and psychotherapy as professions where this would not be out of place, since they deal face to face with their clients and speak *ad hominem*. If a social scientist uses such sentences he is at once identified as a writer (and dismissed).

A writer certainly does not deal *ad hominem* with his unknown readers; yet his readers may take it as if he does and send him letters and so forth.

A writer objectively observes, and so is like a scientist. His method is best compared, in this respect, with natural history or anthropology. A young writer is well advised to learn the geography, botany, and animals—a good model is Hardy—as well as the people and institutions. A writer's method is naturalistic; he does not intervene experimentally or with questionnaires, though like other naturalists, he may station himself to notice what he needs to know.

But then, unlike scientific naturalists, he focuses on the individual case with its unique characteristics, like a painter painting just this scene, or a physician treating just this patient.

He brings together his personal life and the objective subject matter, and the general class and the individual case.

Writers rely heavily on memory, the mother of the muses, both their own biographies and the cultural tradition. Only law, philosophy, and history itself draw as much on records of the past decades, centuries, and millennia. The faculty of bringing together memory and learning with present observation and spontaneous impulse is a remarkable service for human beings. Man is the animal who makes himself and the one who is made by his culture. Literature repeats the meaning and revives the spirit of past makings, so they are not a dead weight, by using them again in a making that is occurring now.

I would not like to distinguish literature from philosophy, if we take philosophy to be the collecting of wide-flung concrete experience, in principle all the experience there is, and saying what is central in it. There are various methods of philosophizing, for instance logical analysis, phenomenological description, grounding and harmonizing the different sciences. Literature could be called philosophizing by making and experimenting with language.

Writers are linguistic analysts and know the folk wisdom and superstition that exist in common vocabulary and grammar. As general semanticists, they are critical of the rhetoric of the street, the mass media, and official institutions. They understand, more than most people, what cannot be said, what is not being said though it ought to be, what is verbalized experience, and what is mere words. They can detect when there is really an idea and an argument rather than a cloud of phrases. They can date a passage and show a forgery. As psychologists of language they are sensitive to how people come on when they talk or write, the ploys they use, and the postures they strike. They can hear the personal character that is expressed in habits of syntax, and the personal inhibition or freedom that is told by the breathing and rhythm of sentences and the quality of metaphor. They can judge the clarity or confusion or spurious clarity in an exposition. They are sociologists of language and

121

can recognize the social background in vocabulary, pronunciation, and routine formulas.

At the same time as they know all this, however, in their own writing they must let their speech come spontaneously; it is free speech, though they monitor it critically. It pursues tangents that they did not plan, produces metaphors that surprise them, uses word order with an emphasis they did not know they had, argues in a way to contradict their theses, and says ideas that they themselves judge to be unpolitical or immoral. But they do not censor or control this wildness, but do their best to assimilate it and keep going. Sometimes the whole must be torn up because it has fallen apart. For writers, these wildnesses are like the phenomena that must be "saved" by the empirical scientist. There are different ideologies to explain the necessity not to control—it is inspiration, it is unconscious contents emerging, the unconscious contents are the return of individual hang-ups, or they are images from the depths, the spontaneous is the voice of the people, or universal man speaking through the writer. Whatever the ideology, a writer writes at the boundary of what he knows.

Not to censor is an act of moral will, a commitment. At some point early in his career a young writer must come to it, like a kind of Hippocratic oath. If he can think something, he will say it; if it says itself, he will not strike it; if he can write it, he will publish it. The writing does not belong to himself.[1] The refusal of censorship and self-censorship is, of course, essential

---

[1]An interesting problem arises with regard to copyright. In principle, what is authentically written is not a commodity bought and paid for, but is in the public domain like air and water and natural growth. Yet as a citizen I object to my writing being exploited for somebody's profit. So I try to set the

for the use of writing against lying and oppressive regimes; but it also makes a writer a thorn in the side of his own political cause: he gets nice about the slogans, he can't say the half-truth, he states the case of the opposition better than is convenient, and so forth. A writer might be a fine citizen in a perfect community, to which he would lend animation; but he is an unreliable ally, he is "unrealistic," in actual politics.

The spontaneity, the free origination, of writing is one aspect of a writer's disinterestedness; he does not will it but he is present with it. The other aspect is as follows.

He writes it *through*, from the beginning through the middle to the end. This is a writer's chief moral virtue, it is an act of will and often requires a lot of fortitude. It is what distinguishes a writer from a dilettante. A young writer is well advised to start on things he can finish and not get bogged down in long novels. By finishing, you learn the habits that work for you and can then set up a bigger structure.

To make a whole work, each sentence follows from the sentence before with "literary probability" and advances the whole, until nothing more follows. In the course of a fairly long work, there are bound to be impasses. The writer must backtrack and choose other alternatives, observe more, and sometimes have bad headaches till he invents something. Here lies the distinction between a good writer and a bad writer. A good writer does not fake it and try to make it appear, to himself or

---

following conditions: if anybody wants to reprint my writing for noncommercial purposes, they can do so gratis; if the State wants to use it, they must give me safeguards; if a commercial enterprise wants to use it, they must pay the going market price.

the reader, that there is a coherent and probable whole when there isn't. If the writer is on the right track, however, things fall serendipitously into place; his sentences prove to have more meaning and formative power than he expected; he has new insights; and the book "writes itself."

At the end of this process, somehow, the finished work will have been worth doing. If it is a long poem, it will have the kind of meaning that poems have. If it is a prose essay, it will say something true about its subject matter.[2]

This last is, of course, simply an act of faith, but it is no different in kind from the faith of all who work at the boundary of the unknown, the faith of a physician that, if he pursues his method, nature will heal the patient; or the faith of an empirical scientist that, if he pursues his method, the nature of things will reveal a secret. Or for that matter, the faith of a child who runs across a field and the ground supports him. If they fail, they do not give up the method, because they have no alternative way of being. When they succeed, they get a passing satisfaction and go on to another work.

Finally there is an odd and revealing unilateral contract that a writer makes with his readers. Some writing, of course, like a

---

[2]Schopenhauer or Nietzsche—I no longer remember which; either is possible because both were snappish and down-to-earth—advises looking first at the last chapter and asking, "*Was will der Mensch?*—What's the man after?" He is after where he ends up. But has he *gone* there? If so, you have to go the way with him. My own usual experience is that I do start out with him frankly on his way; but somewhere along he fakes something, or he doesn't know something that he ought to know; and then I find it hard to continue. My experience also is that one can usually easily recognize the writer who is really in there pitching, suffering, doing his best, finding new things—at least new to himself, and not just working a sewing machine. To him one allows any number of mistakes and gaps.

political tract, an entertainment, or a popularization, is aimed at a particular audience and always keeps them in mind; but much serious writing, perhaps most, is written for no particular audience; and fiction and poetry for an "ideal" audience. Nevertheless, the writer is always under an obligation to make it "clear." He will explain references that an ordinary literate reader is not likely to know, he will fill out the argument, he will avoid private or clique information, even though his ideal audience would hardly need such help. But "clear" does not mean easily comprehensible—consider Mallarmé, an exceedingly clear and logical writer, but one who cannot sacrifice the conciseness, texture, and immediacy of his style just to be easily understood by readers, so you have to figure it out like a puzzle. My opinion is that, in most cases, the writer is not thinking of a reader at all; he makes it "clear" as a contract with *language*. Since it is the essence of speech to have a hearer—even though he intends no hearer—the correct use of speech is to be clear.

Let us go back to the question I started with. How do these traits and powers of literary writing add up to a warrant to make true statements, in the sense that scientific statements are true? They don't. *But there is no alternative.* There is no other discourse but literature that is subjective and objective, general and concrete, spontaneous and deliberate, and that, though it is just thinking aloud, gives so much attention to speech, our chief communication.

Philosophers have always quoted literary texts as if they provided another line of proof, a special kind of evidence. As a writer, I do not judge that I provide evidence. But I do go through the literary process to produce the text.

Men of letters have definite virtues. They do not wear blinders. They are honest and do not omit the seamy or awkward

CRAZY HOPE AND FINITE EXPERIENCE

side. They are intolerant of censorship and skeptical of author-
ity. They work hard to write it through. They disinterestedly
lose themselves in what they do and are innocently in love with
the product.

But it is not so definite what is the use of their ethic. They
are not committed, like scientists, to find confirmable and
replicable truth. Politically, they are usually inept at finding
ways to realize what they advocate. They are not trustworthy as
pedagogues or curers of souls.

Perhaps, in the social division of labor, they are the group to
whom it is assigned to make sense. One is reminded of Nestor,
the orator of the *Iliad*. Nestor's honeyed speech at no time dis-
suaded the Greeks from their infatuation, but it was no doubt a
good thing for them to go to their doom with open eyes.

It has been argued, however, that literature is simply out-
moded in modern times. One clamorous line of attack has recently been coming from the champions of multi-media. In my
opinion it is nonsensical. They say that writing, and indeed all
speech, is "linear," it pays out its meanings one after another like
signals in an unrolling tape. But in fact, speech can be amazingly contrapuntal, more so even than orchestral music with all
its voices and timbres. In colloquial speech, the phonetics,
grammar, and lexicon can simultaneously have meaning, either
reinforcing or shading one another, and to these we must add
non-verbal signs and attending to the respondent. Writing,
which is more deliberate speech, lacks the non-verbal and the
respondent, but it adds contrapuntal voices like a system of
metaphor, systematic irony, allegory, subordination of clauses
in the framework of an independent clause — consider a paragraph of Proust. In poetry it is usual for three systems of rhythm

126

to be heard at the same time, the meter, the beats of phrasing, and the period or paragraph. Good colloquial conversation or the complex-word of a poem can keep globally in touch with almost every aspect of a situation.

Speech rises from within people; they reach out to say it or to hear it, even when they are reading. My observation is that people are rather passive to multi-media. Multi-media have their own quality, of surrounding the audience spatially and sometimes breaking down defenses, but they are not a substitute for saying. It is possible—I doubt it—that future technological and cultural changes may put writing and reading out of business, but other media will not then do the same job as words. It is hard, if at all possible, for non-verbal means to syllogize, define, state class-inclusion, subordinate, say a subjunctive or even imperative or interrogative, to distinguish direct and indirect discourse, to say I, Thou, or It, and so forth. Film, music, and space-arrangements have to use indirect means to communicate these simple things. On this subject, people like McLuhan don't know what they're talking about, though they have other useful things to say. If they would try to write through a book, they would have to make more sense. A written argument won't hang together unless it copes with at least the obvious objections. Putting in a picture doesn't help.

A different objection is to deny that literature as such is relevant, to say that writing is made honest only by its workaday and community use. In its philosophical form, which I remember hearing during the twenties (for example, *Gebrauchsmusik*), this is a profound doctrine. It is close to Goethe's great sentence that "Occasional Poetry is the highest kind"—the poetry of weddings, parties, funerals, and dedications. Street theater and *commedia dell'arte* are the utopia of every playwright. Music and plastic art—though literature less—have certainly flourished in service to religion. It is a doctrine of happy communities.

Since the thirties, however, and very much nowadays, the irrelevance of literature has gotten to mean that the right use of literary speech is political action, like protest songs and guerrilla theater—we simply don't have the community necessary for celebration, occasional poetry, and *commedia dell'arte,* That is, the process of literature is not used in its natural power to find meaning and make sense, so that we can act in a world that has meaning and sense. It is claimed there is no time for this, there is too much suffering and injustice. And only by engaging in revolutionary action can one produce new thought and lively words. But in practice I have found this comes to not questioning slogans that are convenient for an immediate tactic or a transient alliance. The writers tell half-truths. "Action" becomes idiotic activism. The vocabulary and grammar are pitched to a condescending populism, about at the level of junior high school, including the dirty words. The thought is ideological through and through.

There is, finally, a famous analysis of the history of poetry and human speech that in principle makes literature now quite irrelevant. On this view, poetry was the inevitable and appropriate speech of primitive ages, as the only available way of saying reality when not much was known and before the division of labor; these were ages of myth, when people living in a fearful and uncontrollable environment could not distinguish between magic and science, saga and history, dream and empirical experience; the poets were the prophets, historians, philosophers, and scientists. In the course of time, poetry was replaced

128

by philosophy and history; and these in turn have given way to special physical sciences and positivist sociology. In our time, literature can be merely decoration or entertainment or exercises in emotional noises. This was the line of Vico (on one interpretation) and of Comte. And prophylactic empiricist languages, like Basic English or positivist logic, carry it out as a program.

Apologists for literature have tended to regard exactly the same development of language as a devolution rather than an evolution. In his *Defense of Poesie* Philip Sidney argues that history and moral philosophy are ineffectual to teach the man of action and the warrior—he comes on strongly as the Renaissance scholar-poet who is also soldier-statesman. History tells us only what has been, poetry what should be; moral philosophy is dry analysis, poetry motivates to emulation and action. Sidney would certainly not have been happier with the "value-neutral" language of present departments of sociology. In its high Italian form, Sidney's argument goes so far as to deny that scientific or philosophical sentences are true at all; only Eloquence is true, for truth resides in right action, not in propositions, just as Nietzsche holds that the only true science is the *Gaya Scienza* that makes you happy if you know it.

Shelley, in *Defence of Poetry*, takes the same tack. He sees the world of his time as fragmented, quantified, rule-ridden; it is only poetry that can liberate and bring the parts together.

> The great secret of morals is love, or a going out of our own nature and an identification of ourselves with the beautiful which exists in thought, action, or person....A man, to be greatly good, must imagine intensely and comprehensively....Poetry enlarges the circumference of the imagination by replenishing

it with thoughts of ever new delight, which have the power of attracting and assimilating to their own nature all other thoughts.

...We want the creative faculty to imagine that which we know...our calculations have outrun conception....The cultivation of those sciences which have enlarged the limits of the empire of man over the external world has, for want of the poetical faculty, proportionately circumscribed those of the internal world.

In my opinion, there is a lot of truth in this—it is grounded in Coleridge's post-Kantian epistemology. It *is* odd, however, that as a philosophic anarchist after Godwin, Shelley should end his *Defence* with the fatuous sentence, "Poets are the unacknowledged legislators of the world." What does he intend? That they should be acknowledged? Then what would they do?

Depressed by the passing of Faith, Matthew Arnold—in *Literature and Dogma, Culture and Anarchy*, and the debate with Huxley—deplores the language of the churchmen, the Liberal and Radical economists, and the scientists, and he turns desperately to literature to give a standard for "Conduct" for the majority of mankind. Astoundingly, this view has condemned him as an elitist—in a speech by Louis Kampf of MIT, the President of the Modern Language Association! But Arnold is explicitly drawing on the Wordsworthian doctrine that uncorrupted common speech, heightened by passion and imagination, binds mankind together, whereas the utilitarian speech of the Liberals or the ideological speech of the Radicals destroys humanity.

Nearer to our own times, bureaucratic, urbanized, impersonalized, and depersonalized, Martin Buber could no longer rely even on literature, but went back to face-to-face dialogue, the orally transmitted legends of the Hasidim, and the experiences that underlie the text of the Bible. And we see that, in the present deep skepticism about special sciences and scientific technology, the young do not trust speech altogether, but only touching or silence.

In this dispute about the evolution of positivist language or the devolution to positivist language, both sides exaggerate—as usual. It is for quite reasonable human purposes that we have developed languages that are more accurately denotative and analytic and simpler in syntax than poetry. But the broader function of literary language, including poetry, also remains indispensable, because we are never exempt from having to cope with the world existentially, morally, and philosophically; and there is always emerging novelty that calls for imagination and poetry.

Consider the worldwide unease about the technology, the social engineering, the specialist sciences, and their positivist value-neutral language. Suddenly, the line of dissent of Blake, Wordsworth, Shelley, William Morris, the symbolists, and the surrealists no longer seems to be the nostalgic romanticism of a vanishing minority, but the intense realism of a vanguard. I have found that I can mention even Jefferson and ruralism without being regarded as a crank. To try to cope with modern conditions by the methods of laboratory science, statistics, and positivist logic has come to seem obsessional, sometimes downright demented, as in the game-strategies for nuclear warfare. As in a dream, people recall that technology is a branch of moral philosophy, with the forgotten criteria of prudence, temperance, amenity, practicality for ordinary use; and they ask for a science that is ecological and modestly naturalistic rather than aggressively experimental. But one cannot *do* moral philosophy, ecology, and naturalism without literary language. It was only a few years ago that C. P. Snow berated literary men for their ignorance of positive science, and now it is only too clear that there is an even greater need for positive scientists who are literary. Unfortunately, since men of letters have for so long let themselves be pushed out, we don't have relevant literary language and topics to say right technology and ecology; our usual literary attempts are apocalyptic, sentimental, out of date, or private.

A physician, for instance, is faced with agonizing dilemmas: euthanasia when novel techniques can keep tissue alive; birth control despite the destiny of a human being as a parental animal; organ transplants and Lord knows what future developments; the allocation of scarce resources between the vital statistics of public health and the maximum of individual health, or mass practice and family practice. How does one spell out the Hippocratic oath in such issues? How can anyone by his own intuition and individual ratiocination, usually in crisis, possibly decide wisely and without anxiety and guilt? Yet there are almost no medical schools that find time for the philosophy of medicine. And we do not have the linguistic analysis, the reasoned description of precedents, the imagined situations, in brief the literature, for such philosophy.

The social sciences have been positivist only during my lifetime, though Comte talked it up a hundred and fifty years ago. Marx was still able to say that Balzac was the greatest of the sociologists. Comte himself was energized by a crazy utopian poetry. Sir Henry Maine, Maitland, Max Weber, and so forth were historians, humanists. Dewey and Veblen were practical philosophers. Freud and Rank came on like novelists and fantasists and posed the problems for anthropology. It is, of course, a matter of opinion whether, after so many lisping centuries, the brief reign of mature positivist sociology has been brilliant.[3]

My hunch is that, despite a few more years guaranteed by big funding, it is moribund, done in by the social critics and the politically engaged of the past decades, who have had something useful to say. As one of the social critics, I can affirm that we are *philosophes*, men of letters.

Humanly speaking, the special sciences and their positivist language have been deeply ambiguous. At their best—it is a splendid best—they have gotten (and deserved) the payoff of the theological virtues of faith, selflessness, and singleminded devotion, and of the moral virtues of honesty, daring, and accuracy. At their worst, however—and it is a very frequent worst—specialist science and its value-neutral language are an avoidance of experience, a narrow limitation of the self, and an act of bad faith. They are obsessional, an idolatry of the System of Science rather than a service to the unknown God and therefore to mankind. Needless to say, such science can be

---

[3]A recent study captained by Karl Deutsch, emanating from the University of Michigan, points to the great advances in recent years made by big teams of scholars heavily financed; and it refers sarcastically to those—namely me—who claim that we don't know much more than the ancients did about psychology, pedagogy, politics, or any other field where they had adequate empirical evidence. When I look at the list of great advances, however, I find them heavily weighted toward methodology and equipment; stochastic models, computer simulation, large-scale sampling, game theory, structural linguistics, cost-benefit analysis, and so forth; in brief, an enormous amount of agronomy and farm machinery and field hands, but few edible potatoes.

easily bought by money and power. Its language is boring because what the men do is not worth the effort, when it is not actually base. Being busy-work and form-ridden, it has no style.

I have written forty books. Evidently, to make literature is my way of being in the world, without which I would be at a loss. If I here examine and write the Apology for this behavior, I find that it is not very different from the older Defences of Poetry, but I do not need to make their exaggerated claims since I am just describing my own situation—maybe it is simply that Sidney and Shelley were 30 years old, and I am 60.

I have a scientific disposition, in a naturalistic vein. I get a continual satisfaction from seeing, objectively, how things are and work—it makes me smile, sometimes ruefully—and I like to write it down. But I do not exclude how I myself am and work as one of the things, unfortunately an omnipresent one in my experience. (I can occasionally smile at this too, but I am happier when I am not there.) God is history, how events actually turn out; but history includes also the history of me. God creates the world and I am only a creature, but I *am* a creature and He takes me into account, though He doesn't always know what's good for me and I complain a lot. Thus, my objective naturalistic sentences are inevitably colored by, and likely distorted by, my own story and feelings. They turn into literature.

I cannot take my wishes, feelings, and needs for granted and directly try to act them, as many other people seem to be able to do. I have to try to make sense, that is, to say my feelings and needs to myself and to other people. It is no doubt the sign of a deep anxiety; I cannot manage the callousness of healthy good conscience, though I do not feel much conscious guilt. I have to justify my needs with meanings. Conversely, I try to translate into action the meanings that I say, for, as with everybody else, much of the meaning that I know is unsatisfactory and something should be done about it. This combination of action and meaning also results in a lot of literature, rhetoric, social criticism, psychoanalysis, pedagogy, and press conferences.

Whether by nature or long habit that has become second nature, I have that kind of personality that first says and then initiates what it wants, and then knows what it wants, and then wants it. Before saying, I feel just a vague unrest. With most people, it is wise to take seriously what they do, not what they say; their words are rationalizations, pious platitudes, or plain hypocrisy. But writers' words commit them, marshal their feelings, put them on the spot. I make a political analysis because I have a spontaneous gift for making sense; I then have to go through with the corresponding political exercise, unwillingly not because I am timid but because I am lousy at it. I tentatively say "I love you" and find that I love you. Or very often I have said what seems to me to be a bluff, beyond what I know or want, and it proves to be after all what I mean. Like the Egyptian god that Otto Rank mentions, a writer makes himself by saying.

I am in exile. Like everybody else, I live in a world that is given to me—I am thankful for it. It is not made by me—and that too is very well. But it is *not* my native home—therefore I make poems. "To fashion in our lovely English tongue a somewhat livelier world, I am writing this book"—*The Empire City*. In order to appropriate this unfeeling bitter place where I am a second-class citizen. I was no happier when I was young, and I wrote poems; it is no bed of roses when I am toothless and have failing eyes, and I write poems. I never was a beauty, to get what I wanted sexually, but now I am also too tired to seek for it. But

135

even worse than my private trouble is how men have made of the earth an object of disgust, and the stupidity and pettiness of statesmen tormenting mankind and putting additional obstacles in the way, as if life were not hard enough. It does not help, either, that people are so pathetic, the apparently powerful as much as powerless. To pity is another drain of spirit. But it helps me to say it just as it is, however it is.

Also, I am good at thinking up little expedients of how it could be otherwise. I tend not to criticize, nor even to notice, until I can imagine something that would make more sense. My expedients are probably not workable in the form I conceive them, and I certainly do not know how to get them adopted — they are utopian literature — but they rescue me from the horror of metaphysical necessity, and I hope they are useful for my readers in the same way. When they are neat solutions, they make a happy comic kind of poetry. Maybe they are all the more charming because they are practical, simpleminded, and impossible. It is the use of comic writing.

Meaning and confusion are both beautiful. What is chilling is great deeds that have no meaning, the stock-in-trade of warriors and statesmen, but my radical friends also go in for them. What is exasperating is positivistic clarity and precision that are irrelevant to the real irk. A value of literature is that it can inject confusion into positivistic clarity, bring the shadows into the foreground.

Ancient and modern writers are my closest friends, with whom I am in sympathy. They are wise and talented and their conversation sends me. Maybe I am lonely more than average — how would I know? — but I need them. Books and artworks are extraordinary company — one does not need to make allowances!—and in the nature of the case, they speak more clearly to us writers and artists because we respond to them most actively; we notice how he does that, and if it is congenial we say, "I could do something like that." Despite its bloodlessness, the tradition of literature is a grand community and, much as I envy the happy and the young, I doubt that they have as good a one. (How would I know?) Freud said that artists, giving up animal satisfaction and worldly success for their creative life, hope by this detour to win money, fame, and the love of women. He was wrong—I never had such a hope—but I have thereby entered a company that has given me many beautiful hours. Often, talking to young people at their colleges, when I quote from great writers whom I evidently treat as familiars, they look at me with envy because I have a tradition which they lack, through no fault of theirs, but I do not know how to pass it on.

And what a thing it is to write English sentences!—rapid in thought, sometimes blunt, sometimes sinuous in syntax. When writing, I take my syntax and words from my colloquial speech; I strongly disapprove of the usual distinction between "standard colloquial" and "standard literary." I will write the slang that I consider worth using when I talk, for instance in the last few pages I have written "he comes on strongly," "their conversation sends me," "I am lousy at it," "he talked it up." I have no doubt that my voice can be heard in my writing by those who know me face to face. Lecturing, I just muse along and think aloud in a conversational tone, referring to a few notes I have jotted down. When I read verse aloud, I again use a conversational tone and follow the ongoing prose sense rather than the sonority, meter, imagery, or drama. I do not try to be portentous—

Say my song simply for its prosy sentence,
cutting at the commas, pausing at the periods.

Any poetry in it will then be apparent,
motion of mind in English syntax.

On the other hand, though I follow the sense, I am *not* intent on conveying any truth or message, but just the beginning, middle, and end of a whole literary work. I will strike whatever impedes or detracts from the whole, regardless of the "truth." For what I communicate must, in the end, be not anything I know but how I do in getting *rid* of the poem, putting it out there. Afterward, God help me, I am left so much the less.

I use the word "God" freely when I write—much less freely when I speak—never when I think or talk to myself. I don't know clearly what I intend by it. I cannot pray in the usual sense, though I sometimes use the awareness-exercises of psychotherapy which, I guess, is my religion. But in writing of the fundamental relations of my soul, mankind, and the world, I find the terminology of St. Thomas or Karl Barth far more congenial and accurate than that of Freud or Reich, who are either too "subjective" or too "objective," they do not say how it is. To say deliberately just how it is with me is apparently how I pray, if I may judge by the language that comes to me. Especially when I am at a loss for grief, confusion, gratitude, or fear. In moments of impasse—but only when I have earned the right to say it because I have tried hard—I have written "Creator Spirit, come."

Maybe it is that when I think or talk to myself, I am embarrassed, but when I write I am not embarrassed. I now remember that I fell on my knees and said a prayer when I had finished writing *The Empire City*, and indeed the ending of that book is very good.

When I write public themes—urbanism, psychology, delinquency, the school system, the use of technology, resisting the draft—I of course try to be honest with the facts, to "save the phenomena," but again I rather obviously put more trust in the literary process, the flow of saying my say, than in statistics. I take the statistics seriously when they contradict me; I modify my line or make a distinction, or I explain how the statistics are an artifact or haven't asked the right question. I like using abrasive material to work with and I have no impulse to sweep difficulties under the rug. (Sometimes, however, I am simply ignorant.) But when the "facts" run positively in my direction, I do not argue from them but treat them literarily; 85 percent becomes "a good majority," 60 percent is "in very many cases," 35 percent is "an appreciable number of cases," 20 percent is "sometimes it happens that." A single individual situation that I judge to be typical and for which I can provide a global, literary explanation to my satisfaction, weighs more than all the rest, because it is for real and must be coped with politically and humanly. Except for rhetorical effect, I usually don't make generalizations anyway, because I don't care about them—when I do make them they tend to be outrageous because I am outraged. I do not understand a cause or a reason as a correlation, but animally, as continuous with a muscular push or a perceptual Gestalt.

But when I rely on the literary process, the flow of saying my say, this does not mean that I say what I *want* to say but what *can*—strongly—be said. The work has its own discipline, to be clear, to make sense, to hang together, to go from the beginning to the end. For instance, I do not allow myself the usual concessive clause, "Although some cases are not so-and-so, yet the majority of cases are so-and-so." Such a construction is stylistically feeble. If there are well-marked exceptions or a single outstanding exception, it is better to find the distinction that explains the exception and to *affirm* it rather than concede it. The difference will then strengthen the explanation of the other cases; it will provide a new reason. Often it provides the best reason, the one I hadn't thought of till I had to write the sentence. A strong and scrupulous style is a method of discovery.

Commenting on this, an unfriendly critic might say, "You mean that it is true if it sounds good." To which I would reply, in an unfriendly tone of voice, "Yes."

My reliance on colloquial speech and the process of literature is certainly closely related, whether as cause or effect, to my political disposition. I am anarchistic and agitational, and I am conservative and traditional. So is good speech. Insistently and consistently applied, any humane value, such as common sense, honor, honesty, or compassion, will soon take one far out of sight of the world as it is; and to have meaning is one of the virtues that is totally disruptive of established institutions. Nevertheless, meaningful language and coherent syntax are always historical and traditional and always have a kind of logic. Speaking is a spontaneous action of the speaker, and he speaks only in a community, for a hearer. Colloquial speech cannot be regimented, whereas even perception and science can be regimented—perception because it is passive, science because they can put blinders on it like a directed horse. But the vulnerability of colloquial speech, unfortunately, is that its freedom is limited to where the speakers have initiative, eyewitnessing,

and trust, and these limits may be made narrow indeed. The literary process expands these limits by historical memory, international culture, and welcoming the dark unconscious which
common folk prudently inhibit. Common speech can be pretty
empty and aimless, whereas to write you must know at least
something and try to be clear—it is a profession.

Slogans can't last long in either common speech or literature. In revolutionary situations, the new people, making bad
literature (and sometimes even writing it down), have to recall
ancient languages, as the Reformers picked up the Hebrew pa-
triarchs, the French Revolutionists picked up Marcus Brutus,
and the hippies pick up various Indians and Amerindians; but
the good writers ridicule these too.

Thus, my Apology for the literature to which I have devoted
the years of my life is very like the others over several centuries,
and it is noteworthy that they are all similar. Possibly if we had
a very different kind of community, we would say something
different; but possibly it is the human condition—how would
I know? Literature confounds the personal and impersonal,
meaning and beginning to act, and thought and feeling. In this
confusion which is like actual experience, it makes a kind of
sense. It imagines what might be, taking account of what is.
Using the code of language, it continually revises the code to
cope with something new. It is more conservative than science
and more daring than science. It makes the assured and powerful uneasy, if only out of powerless spite. It speaks my common
speech and it makes human speech noble. It provides a friendly
community across ages and boundaries, and cheers my solitude.
It is the way I pray to God and patriotically revere my background. It is legitimacy and rebellion.

The Editor

TAYLOR STOEHR is Paul Goodman's literary executor and is writing Goodman's biography. Born in Omaha, Nebraska in 1931, Taylor Stoehr attended the public schools there, and received his B.A. degree (1952) from the University of Omaha. He studied at the University of California, Berkeley, where he received his Ph.D. degree (1960) in English and American literature. He has taught at Cornell University, the State University of New York, Buffalo, and the University of California, Santa Cruz. Since 1971 he has been Professor of English at the University of Massachusetts, Boston.

In addition to editing over a dozen volumes of Goodman's work, Stoehr has also written five books and many articles on such literary figures as Dickens, Lawrence, Hawthorne, and Thoreau, as well as cultural studies of utopian communities, the free love movement, pseudoscience, and other countercultural experiments in nineteenth-century America. His most recent books are *Decentralizing Power*, a collection of Paul Goodman's social criticism, *Format and Anxiety*, a collection of Paul Goodman's writings on the media, and *Here Now Next: Paul Goodman and the Origins of Gestalt Therapy*, a study of Goodman's

143

collaboration with Frederick (Fritz) Perls in the founding of a new psychotherapeutic movement.

Taylor Stoehr has five children and a stepson. He lives in Cambridge, Massachusetts, with his wife, the feminist scholar Ruth Perry.